IN THE SAME ORIGINAL FORMAT, GENERAL EDITOR AND DESIGNER DAVID BROWER:

This Is the American Earth, by Ansel Adams and Nancy Newhall
Words of the Earth, by Cedric Wright
These We Inherit: The Parklands of America, by Ansel Adams
"In Wildness Is the Preservation of the World," by Eliot Porter
The Place No One Knew: Glen Canyon on the Colorado, by Eliot Porter
The Last Redwoods: Photographs and Story of a Vanishing Scenic Resource, by
    Philip Hyde and Francois Leydet
Ansel Adams: A Biography. Volume I: The Eloquent Light, by Nancy Newhall
Time and the River Flowing: Grand Canyon, by Francois Leydet
Gentle Wilderness: The Sierra Nevada, text from John Muir,
    photographs by Richard Kauffman
Not Man Apart: Photographs of the Big Sur Coast,
    with lines from Robinson Jeffers
The Wild Cascades: Forgotten Parkland, by Harvey Manning,
    with lines from Theodore Roethke
Everest: The West Ridge, by Thomas F. Hornbein, with
    photographs from the American Mount Everest Expedition
Summer Island: Penobscot Country, by Eliot Porter
Navajo Wildlands: As Long as the Rivers Shall Run, photographs by
    Philip Hyde, text by Stephen Jett, edited by Kenneth Brower
Kauai and the Park Country of Hawaii, by Robert Wenkam
    edited by Kenneth Brower
Glacier Bay: The Land and the Silence, by Dave Bohn
Baja California and the Geography of Hope, photographs by Eliot Porter,
    text by Joseph Wood Krutch, edited by Kenneth Brower
Central Park Country: A Tune Within Us, photographs by Nancy and Retta
    Johnston, text by Mireille Johnston, introduction by Marianne Moore
Galapagos: The Flower of Wildness (both volumes edited by Kenneth Brower)
1. *Discovery*, photographs by Eliot Porter, introduction by Loren Eiseley,
    with selections from Charles Darwin, Herman Melville, and others; and
2. *Prospect*, photographs by Eliot Porter, introduction by John P. Milton,
    text by Eliot Porter and Kenneth Brower

THE EARTH'S WILD PLACES
Maui: The Last Hawaiian Place, by Robert Wenkam,
    edited, with Kipahulu Sketches, by Kenneth Brower
Return to the Alps, by Max Knight and Gerhard Klammet,
    edited, with selections from Alpine literature, by David R. Brower
The Primal Alliance, Earth and Ocean, by John Hay and Richard Kauffman,
    edited by Kenneth Brower
Earth and the Great Weather: The Brooks Range, by Kenneth Brower
Eryri, the Mountains of Longing, by Amory Lovins,
    with photographs by Philip Evans, edited by David R. Brower
A Sense of Place: The Artist and the American Land, by Alan Gussow,
    with illustrations by fifty-nine painters, and foreword by Richard Wilbur
Micronesia: Island Wilderness, by Kenneth Brower and Robert Wenkam
Guale, the Golden Coast of Georgia, James P. Valentine, Robert Hanie,
    Eugene Odom, John P. Milton *et al.*, edited by Kenneth Brower

Endpaper   *Bog moss (Sphagnum)*

RETURN TO THE ALPS

I tried to let their beauty soak in,

and when I did so a new beauty, something additional
to all I had yet seen, seemed to shine out of them;
out of the grass an added richness of green,
out of the pines more fragrance of resin,
from the blossoms a glow of color still brighter;

Kreuzeck near Garmisch, view toward Zugspitze

unfathomable deeps and gentleness
bloomed in the sky's blue.
This newness taken on by the world
was like that of something freshly created.

                                                        . . .

Its loveliness had youth and vigor and an immortality
so obviously not of its manifested self,

but of that ever new and ancient beauty,
wherein all individual things have being and life,
and which they serve.

. . .

Alpine brook

Five thousand feet under me, from the dark greens of the gorge
up to the brown tip of the bird's wings,
turned to the sky where it wheeled in thin pure air,
and in all that lay between,
there was displayed the overwhelming beauty of things
sharply strange and separate,
that from their beginning were entered into one another and oned.

. . .

*How clearly this integrating principle of the universe
disposed and flung forth His power that morning.
His name men called God, or the Infinite One, Beauty or Truth,
according to the context in which His works happen to be seen.*

W. H. MURRAY

by Max Knight

photographs by Gerhard Klammet

RETURN TO THE ALPS

edited, with a foreword and
selections from Alpine literature,
by David R. Brower

FRIENDS OF THE EARTH ⊕ SAN FRANCISCO, NEW YORK, LONDON, PARIS
A CONTINUUM BOOK / THE SEABURY PRESS NEW YORK

We are grateful for permission to reprint excerpts from these books:

Eiseley, Loren, *The Immense Journey*, New York, Random House, Inc., 1957.

Gesner, Conrad, *On the Admiration of Mountains*, San Francisco, The Grabhorn Press, 1937.

Hammarskjöld, Dag, *Markings*, New York, Alfred A. Knopf, copyright © 1964.

Heller, Eric, *The Disinherited Mind*, Cambridge, England, Bowes and Bowes, 1952.

Keyserling, Count Hermann, *The Travel Diary of a Philosopher*, New York, Harcourt, Brace and Co., copyright © 1925.

Krutch, Joseph Wood, *Grand Canyon Today and All Its Yesterdays*, New York, William Sloane Associates, 1958.

Muir, John, *Mountains of California*, London, T. Fisher Unwin, 1894.

———, *My First Summer in the Sierra*, Boston, Houghton Mifflin Company, 1911 by John Muir.

Murray, W. H., *The Scottish Himalayan Expedition*, London, J. M. Dent and Sons, 1951.

Ortega y Gasset, José, *The Dehumanization of Art and Notes on the Novel*, Princeton, Princeton University Press, copyright © 1948.

Pope Pius XI *in* Captain John Noel's *The Story of Everest*, Boston, Little, Brown and Company, copyright © 1927.

Rébuffat, Gaston, *Mont Blanc to Everest*, London, Thames and Hudson, 1956; French edition published by B. Arthaud, Grenoble.

Rey, Guido, *Peaks and Precipices*, New York, Dodd, Mead and Company, 1914.

Rousseau, Jean-Jacques, *Reveries of a Solitary*, Routledge & Sons, London, 1927 (translated by John Gould Fletcher).

Smythe, F. S., *The Valley of Flowers*, New York, W. W. Norton, 1949.

Thoreau, Henry David, *The Maine Woods*, New York, Thomas Y. Crowell and Co., 1906.

Tietjens, Eunice, "The Most Sacred Mountain," 1917, *in* Edwin O. Grover, ed., *The Nature Lover's Knapsack*, New York, T. Y. Crowell, copyright © 1947.

Tolkien, J. R. R., *The Lord of the Rings*, Vols. I and II, Boston, Houghton Mifflin Company, © 1954.

Young, Geoffrey Winthrop, *On High Hills*, London, Methuen and Co., Ltd., 1927.

———, *Mountains with a Difference*, London, Eyre & Spottiswoode, 1951.

ISBN 0-913890-05-7

Printed and bound in Italy

This Friends of the Earth/Seabury Press printing contains corrections of minor errors but no substantive changes in text, photographs, or other illustrations. For current information about what is happening in the earth's wild places, write Friends of the Earth, San Francisco.

Lake Plan, Tirol

at home what kind of development there would be in their favorite places in the Sierra wilderness if developers of the Alps had enjoyed a free hand. I exported Alpine trails, roads, power development, buildings, and mining to the Sierra, and fortifications as well:

"Forts are everywhere, too—on canyon bottoms, high on the canyon walls, built into commanding peaks. . . . Had they been manned toward the close of the Italian campaign, when the 10th Mountain Division, leading others in this theater, were exploiting their Po Valley gains by beating most of the Germans to the Alpine passes, someone else would surely have had to write this piece."

I listed two simple steps by which a wilderness could be killed:

"1. Improve and exploit it. Keep adding the comforts that each preceding addition has brought people to demand. *Procedure:* Build another trail. The users will want a shelter hut. Build that. The guest will want food and drink, hot and cold running water, light. Then he'll want more room for friends. Or supply the site by plane, and sooner or later you will have a clientele with the same demands. Obviously a road will be needed right to the spot, then beyond it to link with another road of similar origin. The game preserve the road cuts will shrivel from the wound, but will only be reduced in effective game refuge by about fifty per cent. The process may have to be repeated to destroy it utterly. Now you have a newly accessible region that just cries for development. Jobs will be created. . . .

"2. Rely always on the apparently democratic argument that you must produce the greatest good for the greatest number. Chances are no man will call to your attention that irreplaceable treasures are destroyed if they are divided or trampled—that no one would think of cutting into little bits, so that all could enjoy them, Michelangelo's frescoes in the Sistine Chapel. And obviously, you can tell him, the wilderness is very big. . . .

"But don't let him ask you what his children, and theirs, are going to do when they want to see for themselves how wild places used to look before man decided to help God keep them."

That very question was being asked more and more insistently, I learned after I returned to California. The Wilderness Society and the Sierra Club held a series of wilderness conferences that led, after fifteen years' effort, to a National Wilderness Preservation System.

In the 1957 conference, Professor Starker Leopold remembered his father, Aldo Leopold's, lines, "Recreational development is a job not of building roads into lovely country, but of building receptivity into the still unlovely human mind," and saw a chance of success: "We owe it to ourselves and to the good earth that supports us to curb our avarice to the extent of leaving a few spots untouched and unexploited. . . . I think that [future philosophers] may put their finger on this century as a time of outstanding advance in man's feeling of responsibility to the earth."

If this feeling advanced more swiftly in the United States than in other countries, it was for a reason not to be proud of: in the U.S., an enormous heritage of wilderness was destroyed so quickly that there was no doubt who the destroyers were or of the need to flag them down. Elsewhere the erosion is slow—or used to be. Now, in the Alps the last wild islands are going rapidly enough to catalyze a defense. We hope these pages will help this feeling of responsibility to the Alps grow swiftly.

Max Knight's perspective of his hills of home is a very personal story of what a man sees who does not get home as often as he would like to, who is only an occasional mountaineer, and then not the seeker after the great walls and needles. His Alps are the gentler Alps, and for that reason the more easily lost. Gerhard Klammet has searched out the same kind of mood, and has done it beautifully. Anthony Knight, who must live longer with what happens, wants the right things to happen, and makes no bones about the rush to overdevelopment. Several interludes explore into what the Alps have meant to many men, and what men brought there to make them a playground, but a decreasingly beautiful playground as more emphasis was placed on what was brought and less on what was there to begin with. There are voices from many lands, not always voices from mountaineers, and several from nonresidents.

It is not fitting for the visitor to tell the visited much more than thank you for the beautiful things seen. It is fitting, however, for people who are trying to keep American wilderness from being mechanized to look critically at what American money has done, or may be doing, to Alpine wilderness. *Austrian Information*, the Austrian govment's public-relations bulletin published in New York, reported in January 1967, "One of the most important aspects of financing the Austrian tourist facility improvements has been the European Recovery Plan (Marshall Plan) Counterpart Fund loans; $25 million have been granted for construction of skiing facilities alone." The 1968 *Oesterreichisches Jahrbuch*, an official publication comparable to the Statistical Yearbook in the United States, says, "Austria received 150 million schillings in ERP credits; 1.2% of these were for skilifts." And, back to *Austrian Information*, January 1967: "Kaprun, Austria's most famous, largest, and most beautiful hydroelectric plant was constructed largely from Marshall Plan funds.''

Enterprise less well intended was remarked upon long ago by the Mexican, Castro, before an assembly in Monterey, California, when the state was still ruled by Mexico: "These Americans are so contriving that some day they will build ladders to touch the sky, and once in the heavens they will change the whole face of the universe and even the color of the stars.''

A world that is running out of wilderness needs a new approach. Overdevelopment is old hat now. The Friends of the Earth series, The Earth's Wild Places, has been created in coöperation with the John Muir Institute for Environmental Studies to seek new approaches. Wilderness is an essential part of the earth's diversity, and diversity is an essential part of what lets life go on, including man's life. We have enjoyed the valuable support of many organizations in getting this series under way, notably from The Conservation Foundation, the International Union for the Conservation of Nature and Natural Resources, and the Sierra Club. If it will help the Alps to continue to be finished in beauty, Friends of the Earth, with such facilities as the organization has here and abroad, will endeavor to extend the kind of support it has received. The Alps are part of our geography of hope, no matter what land we live in. We want never to grow tired of each other.

Added to the pleasure of working on anything that has to do with the Alps, we are grateful for the contribution the Knights, father and son, and Gerhard Klammet have made to the second volume of our series. I myself am grateful for the wealth of material that arrived, when I asked for quotations from mountaineering literature that had turned them on, from fellow Sierra Club members whose nominations I have drawn upon in the Interludes: Mrs. Nick (Betsy) Clinch, Eugene Coan, Miss May Dornin, Mrs. Herbert Eloesser, C. M. Larsen, and Eulalia Nyce Walker and Julie Nyce Walker. Special thanks are due Dr. James T. Lester, who brought his psychologist's skills to bear in the longest of the interludes, the interrelated quotations from men who were far removed from each other geographically but not far apart in what they have to say.

To W. H. Murray, whose writing is so important to the opening and closing of this book, my special thanks. His *The Scottish Himalayan Expedition* was sent me for review in 1952 by Howard Zahniser, of The Wilderness Society. Conservation battles intervened consecutively and I never reviewed the book as I should have, and thus treasure my copy illicitly. It has come to hand often for the beauty of its writing and thinking. His lines on commitment have moved many people. We are hoping that his knowledge of the Highlands will soon help serve our series, The Earth's Wild Places. We are grateful too for critical assistance from Edwin Spencer Matthews, Jr., of Paris and Eric Schindler-Pacozzi of Zürich, who are pioneering the Friends of the Earth effort in Europe.

Thanks must go also to the man whose devotion to the literature of mountaineering shows unmistakably in the beautiful Grabhorn book from which the material on Conrad Gesner and the Theuerdank illustrations have come—Francis P. Farquhar, in whose library, over the period of thirty-five years, I learned much about mountains and the people who love them.

DAVID R. BROWER, *Director*
John Muir Institute for Environmental Studies

Berkeley, California
August 21, 1970

Theuerdank
in need of
assistance

Acknowledgments

IT ALL STARTED with a letter to my colleagues at the University of California Press in 1953. In this letter, written during my first return trip to the Alps after fifteen years, I told how it felt to be back. August Frugé, director of the Press and then editor of the *Sierra Club Bulletin*, suggested that I write a full article about my experience; it appeared under the title "Return to the Alps" in the June 1954 issue of the bulletin—to become, years later in revised form, the introductory pages of the present book. The article found a friendly reception—with George Marshall who had a manuscript on a related subject and invited me to participate in its publication (*Arctic Wilderness*, 1956; republished as *Alaska Wilderness*, 1970); with Raymond Cowles who had a manuscript related in its wildlife aspects to Marshall's, and in the publication of which I participated also (*Zulu Journal*), 1959; and with David Brower who, fourteen years after the appearance of the article, still remembered it and encouraged me to go further yet—by writing this book. In 1968, as Executive Director of the Sierra Club, Dave invited me to take part in manning the club's book exhibit at the Frankfurt International Book Fair. There, one exciting evening, he masterminded the idea of this book, to become, together with *Maui*, one of the two opening volumes in a new series about the world's wild places. Dave's enthusiasm, supported by Perry Knowlton and David Hales, was infectious, and so I signed a hand-written agreement—we didn't have a typewriter at the time. It was also at Frankfurt that we were fortunate enough to meet Gerhard Klammet whose masterful photographs fascinated us at once.

In the text I acknowledge my debt to other authors by citing their works, but I would like to single out here some that I found particularly useful. Among the classics I drew especially on Leslie Stephen, *The Playground of Europe* (1871) and W. A. B. Coolidge, *The Alps in Nature and History* (1908); more recent sources were Gavin de Beer, *Alps and Men* (1932) and *Alps and Elephants* (1955); Claire E. Engel, *A History of Mountaineering in the Alps* (1950), Vivian H. Green, *The Swiss Alps* (1961), Arnold Lunn, *The Swiss and Their Mountains* (1963; along with his earlier books, *The Explorations of the Alps*, 1914, and *The Englishman in the Alps*, 1927); and a number of recent guidebooks (such as Eugene Fodor's *Modern Guides: Switzerland*) and recent Alpine journals.

Among the personal debts: Heinz Stremayr of the Oesterreichischer Alpenverein in Innsbruck was a reliable and competent friend when I needed information. Gerhard Klammet in Garmisch-Partenkirchen was helpful beyond the call of his illustrating duties. My friends and colleagues, Jennie Burton, Joseph Fabry, Erika Hublitz, and Lucy Lawrence, read the manuscript with benevolent relentlessness saving me embarrassments concerning facts and style, for which I am blushingly thankful. Dave Brower, of course, is more than an editor of the volume: he conceived it, designed it, made the layout, had the final word in the selection and presentation of the pictures, chose the quotations that serve as legends—and proved to me by a merciless map that Mont Blanc, at 15,782 feet, is not Europe's highest peak as I had thought; it's Elbrus in the Caucasus: 18,481 feet.

Virginia Herrick of Sunnyvale, California, drew the map, patiently adding ever new names to the Alpine chain as the writing of the story progressed. And Eula Jackson kept the midnight electricity burning, faithfully typing away against a threatening deadline.

To one and all my warm thanks.

This is a personal book, not a guide to the Alps. It is a loose collection of episodes remembered by one who loves the mountains, combined with such spots of background as seemed appropriate or interesting. I did not attempt to explore the Alps systematically. Some areas I never visited; others I visited several times—when I felt that they were inviting me back. I did not try to "cover" all aspects or areas of the Alps. Many that are considered "must-sees" I have not seen. Leslie Stephen, a British nineteenth-century Alpinist, is my excuse. He was tolerant of those "who set the established code of sightseers at defiance—to go to America without seeing the falls of Niagara, or to go to Rome without seeing St. Peter's, or to Jerusalem without seeing the Holy Sepulchre." Although I have not seen all the Alps, I want to write about them, and I invoke Henry James' excuse for writing of Venice: "I hold any writer sufficiently justified who is himself in love with his theme."

M.K.

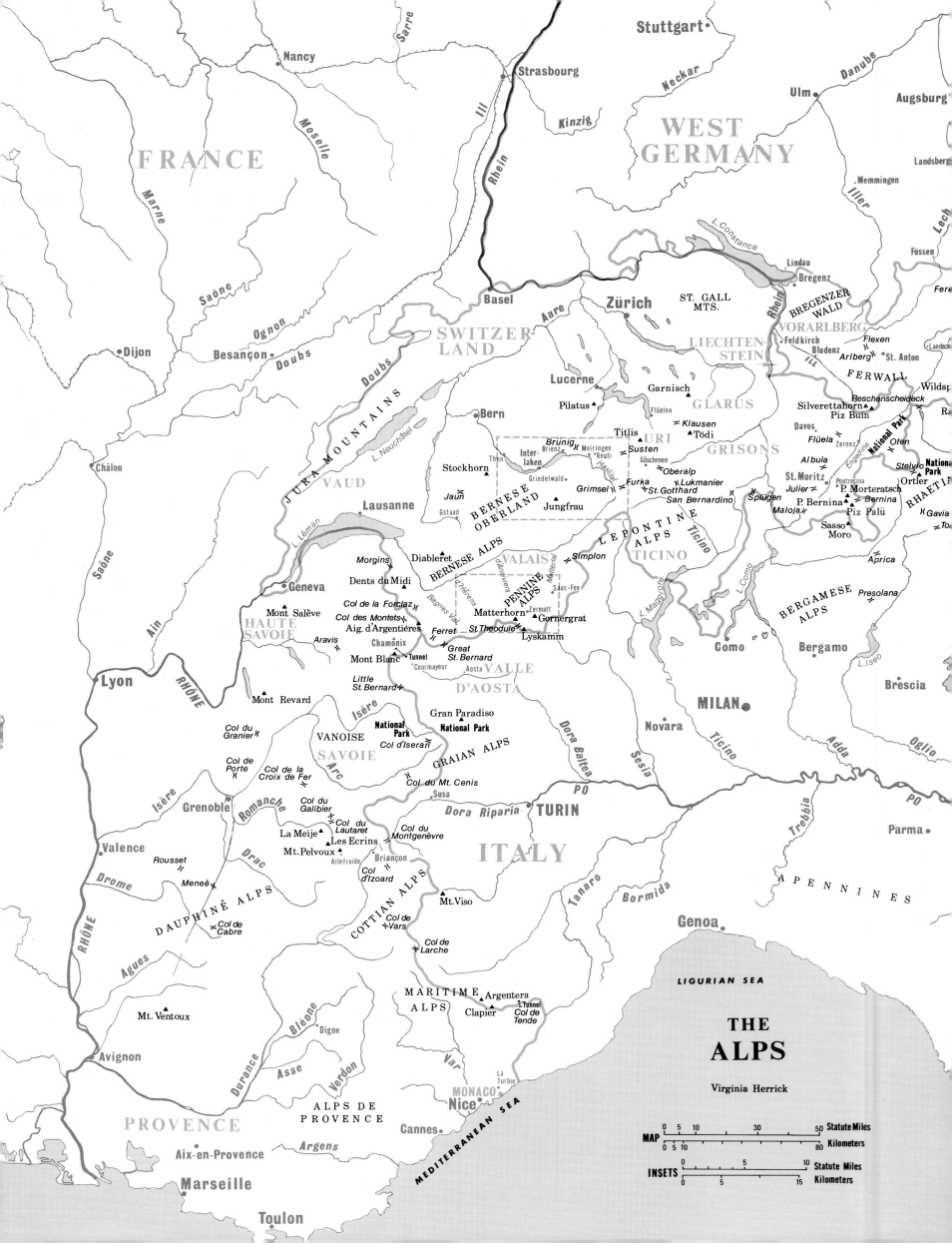

THE
ALPS

Virginia Herrick

1. Return to the Alps

I HAD NOT SEEN the Alps for fifteen years.

When I was four years old my father rolled my jacket, my windbreaker, and my lunch in a bundle and stuffed them into a tiny rucksack which, from then on, I was to carry myself when we hiked in the Vienna Woods. When I was five I got my first Lederhosen to take the place of my short linen pants.

When I was seventeen I stood on a high Tirolean mountain, with a heavy rucksack, a pair of Lederhosen greasy from years of hiking in the Alps, a sprig of Alpenrosen pinned to my jacket. A dirndl-skirted girl sat beside me, barefoot, her hands clasped around her knees. The grass of the mountain meadow was short and mossy and had the feel of a bearskin. With sun-flushed faces we looked toward the peaks, breathing the cold, fresh air.

When I was eighteen I hitchhiked to Switzerland, heading for the myth-shrouded Matterhorn, which for years I had longed to see. On the way a motorist offered me a ride to the Dolomites, a temptation I could not resist. So I allowed myself to get sidetracked, trusting I would see the Matterhorn another time. I did—about forty years later.

After I had made my home in California and the years had passed, the memory of Austria faded—except for the Alps. I made trips to many lands, visiting many peers of the Alps—Canada's proud Rockies, Japan's venerable Fujiyama, California's magnificent Sierra. But although my Lederhosen were locked in a basement trunk, the memory of the Alps lived on.

Occasionally, when I admitted I was thinking of the Alps—the Vienna Woods, Tirol, the Matterhorn—friends would tell me that I was just yearning for bygone youth. Many a Sunday I drove a few hours in search of a small green patch for a family picnic—a patch, that is, with grass grown naturally, not coaxed into existence by a sprinkler system in a public park. I thought about the lush *Almen*, the "alps" in the original sense of the word, the pastures of the Alps. They became a neverland of green.

And then, one postwar summer, I was looking straight at them. For three hours the Arlberg Express sped along in that blessed land as I stood by the window watching the changing scene.

It was a common enough experience—seeing old places again. I had decided to live, for once and for a short time, a life given completely to the elementary joys that come from natural beauty, sunshine, trees, undisturbed by as much as a newspaper. So often in years past had I heard people say, when they talked about the anxieties and responsibilities of daily life, how wonderful it would be if sometime they could "forget it all." Really doing just that was the only uncommon thing about my trip.

As I stood by the train window I realized that although I had remembered the grass, I had forgotten the flowers. The train followed a green land dotted with millions of buttercups and foxgloves and larkspurs and snapdragons and wild pansies and bellflowers and cornflowers and red poppies and daisies and many others whose names I did not know in English. Hour after hour these welcoming flowers would be with me in a never-ending band, and I greeted them affectionately as I rode along. Weeks later, when I was up in those mountains that were now visible in the distance, I would come across people who asked me why I had picked weeds along with my flowers. I did not explain that they were not weeds to me, but friends whom I had not seen for a long time.

The mountains squeezed the narrow flowery land between them. We rode in a valley between the peaks. They had snowy caps, and from them wild foaming brooks tumbled down. You could almost feel how cold they were.

The green lane was paralleled by a country road. We passed a number of Leiterwagen—horse-drawn wagons with racks. Hay was stacked high, and kerchiefed peasant women sitting on top waved to the train. Gabled wooden houses with begonia-decorated, carved balconies appeared and disappeared. No billboard spoiled the scenery.

As we approached Vienna, I greeted every familiar hill of the Vienna Woods. Here was the one where we had our Boy Scout headquarters in the quarry; here the one where you could find shell fossils, here the one where we bandaged Lotte's leg when she got caught in barbed wire.

For hours I stood by the open window with wind and sun beating down on my face. When we arrived in Vienna I was as tan as if I had already spent a week in the Alps.

In the morning, before I had unpacked my suitcase, I was on my way to the Kahlenberg in the Vienna Woods. The nearly 800-mile range of the Alps begins in Vienna with these extensions of the foothills of the Alps ("Voralpen") that rise to the Alps proper in Tirol and Switzerland and Italy and France. The Kahlenberg is the first rung of the ladder that comprises the Alps. It is only 1,400 feet high, and still within the metropolitan limits of Vienna.

Beneath me lay the city of Vienna. To the left, the Danube, to the right, the soft rolling hills of the Kobenzl;

Langtauferer glacier and Hochvernagel, Tirol

in front of me, slightly below, the vineyards of Sievering and Grinzing, with a sweep, sweetness, and music that made me understand the inspiration of Schubert and Mozart; in the distance, hazy outlines of Hungarian hills.

As the shadows grew longer I slowly walked up to the Sofienalpe, a neighboring hill. A playground for Vienna's Sunday hikers, it was that day quiet and peaceful and infinitely lovely. The beeches were tall and slender, their nodding crowns forming arches through which to walk. No one was around. The parting sun shot horizontal beams of light through the trees, outlining them as dark silhouettes. This place was a symbol of my childhood; it had determined many of my standards of beauty. I had been here so many times—when I was happy and when I thought I was not, when I felt on top of the world and when my boyish heart was broken. I walked among the trees and between little stumps from which new branches had grown. Last year's fallen leaves formed a soft cover on the ground. Never before had I noticed the delicate fragrance of this place; I had always taken it for granted.

I picked a couple of beech leaves, to be taken to America. As I walked down several twisting trails in the darkness, I did not realize until I reached the bottom of the hills an hour later that not once had I lost my way . . .

From the Vienna Woods I followed the Alps westward into the lake world of the Salzkammergut. I had expected to find St. Wolfgang spoiled by tourists of the fashionable White Horse Inn type, and Ischl by international patients suffering real and imaginary ailments. But I found much of the old pace of life. A bumpety toy train, discontinued since then, took me from Ischl to Salzburg—a distance about the same as from San Francisco to Sacramento. An old bearded peasant got on at one of the stops and was greeted by a young woman in the car.

"Where d'you come from?" asked the man.

"From Ischl."

"Ah—Ischl! Aren't you ambitious! I won't get there in my lifetime anymore. I was there once, when the old Kaiser still lived."

The mountains of the Salzkammergut were rich with memories for me—Dachstein, Traunstein, Totes Gebirge. But they still averaged no more than 5,000 feet, and I had already caught the fever for the higher peaks. The glaciers and the alps of Tirol were beckoning.

I followed the chain of the Alps to Innsbruck, Tirol's capital. At Kitzbühel the bizarre peaks of Wilder Kaiser appeared. The train was full of youthful mountaineers. Many had to stand, and I was among them. But I didn't mind. I wore my old Lederhosen, exhumed from their California basement grave; I felt young, forgetting the years that had passed, as my eyes rested with pleasure upon a young Dirndl of eighteen or so who sat next to where I was standing. She returned my glance, got up, and offered me her seat. That took me down a peg.

The Stubai valley and the Oetz valley are two of several parallel Tirolean mountain valleys, each of which runs at a right angle to the Inn River, a main tributary of the Danube. These Tirolean valleys are not connected; if you want to go from one to the other you have to follow the first down to the Inn, then follow the Inn until you reach the mouth of the second one, then go up. Or you can cross from one valley to the other by climbing the intervening mountains up one side and down the other.

I did that. Joining a small group of tourists, I took several days to cross from the Stubai valley over a 10,000-foot peak into the Oetz valley. It took one day for the leisurely climb to a mountain hut built at the edge of a glacier. We had decided to stay in that hut overnight, then cross the ice-bound top on the second day. We planned to spend the following night in hut number two, built at the opposite side of the glacier, beyond the top, on the way down to the Oetz valley.

I have enjoyed few hours as much as those spent in the ascent to the first hut while rain was falling. It wasn't a downpour, but a refreshing spray, which bothered none of the company in their watertight boots and loden cloaks. I had brought a poncho, which had rendered good service many times in the Sierra, and was duly admired as something rare in the Alps.

The fine rain added to the feeling of freshness from dozens of cold brooks that came down from the glacier we would be crossing tomorrow. Everything around was green and rich and growing abundantly. It was here that I saw the first gentian of this trip—that deep blue, single bell that has become the symbol of the Alps, sharing the affection of mountain climbers only with Edelweiss and Alpenrosen. There are several varieties of gentian. The one we saw was stemless and had a metallic luster inside.

In the evening we arrived in the Alpine Club hut. These huts, owned by the tourist clubs, are usually leased to caretakers.

The woman in charge was busy preparing Kaiserschmarrn—scrambled pancakes—and we ordered some for dinner. The center of the room was taken up by the huge wood stove; it had a rail all around on which woolen socks were hanging to dry; several pairs of hobnailed boots were close against the stove for the same reason. It was dark outside. A bowl of Alpenrosen stood on the table, which was illuminated by a kerosene lamp.

Our guide, Johann Salchner, a Stubai valley native,

roused us from our bunks at 4 A.M. the next day. We poured a little cold water from the china pitcher in the basin and dipped our fingertips into it, going through the motions of a morning wash. It was very cold, and we didn't thaw out until we got to the warm kitchen and ate our fill for the trip.

As we started across the glacier just beyond the hut, the snow was crisp. We took our time, patiently putting one foot in front of the other. After a couple of hours we had left every bit of green and soil behind us. This was the zone of eternal snow. It was an unreal world, with the reflection of light from the snow hitting our eyes despite our dark glasses and despite the fact that the sun was hiding. We walked in single file, the guide ahead carrying rope and ice ax. All around, snow-covered mountains loomed high above us, as we crawled to the top like black beetles.

We reached the summit at noon. It gave us a superb view back into the Stubai valley whence we had come, and ahead into the Oetz valley where we were bound. The glacier on which we stood reached some distance down into the second valley. Where the ice ended we could see hut number two, our goal for the day.

There was an ice-free spot on the summit, swept clean by the wind that was usually blowing over the crest. When we arrived, the sun came out, and we took our shirts and shoes off. Some fine small flowers, like strawberry blossoms, grew here. "Gamskresse," said the guide —plants eaten by chamois.

We spent half the afternoon at the summit. We were in no hurry. As we lay there, at peace with a tranquil world, we were flanked by two chains, the Stubai Alps on one side, the Oetz valley Alps on the other—summit after summit as far as the eye could see. The row of peaks continued endlessly as they accompanied us into our nap.

A short descent in the late afternoon took us to the second hut, where we stayed for the night. Here, we were about a third of the way down into the Oetz valley. The next morning we continued our descent under our own power. The guide returned, having taken us safely across the glacier.

We were now in the lovely country of the Almen, the classic pastureland of the Alps. Soon after leaving the second hut we discovered a bright red spot in the near distance. It was the first shrub of Alpenrosen, an exciting, moving sight. As we descended further, more Alpenrosen appeared, at first in little islands, then in large patches, until finally the whole mountainside was covered with them, cascading down for miles.

After two hours the steep trail flattened out, allowing a small unbridled brook—which had issued from the glacier and had followed us all the way down—to overflow its shallow banks, irrigate the surrounding meadow, and turn this mountain valley into a flower garden. Below us lay the valley with millions of colored dots strewn in the pasture; left and right, the mountainsides enclosing the valley were covered with Alpenrosen in full bloom; at the foot of the valley, a white foaming stream wound its way; above us, the tops of the snow-covered Stubai Alps looked over one end of the valley, those of the Oetz valley Alps over the other; in the center, cuddled against a small knoll, was hut number three.

We were halfway down to the Oetz valley. Two of us decided to stay in hut number three for a few days. The rest went on.

If the Lord is black for Africans, heaven is green for Austrians. I closed my eyes and tried to remember how I had dreamed about some mountain Shangri-la as I had known it in my childhood. On my way to Europe I had prepared myself for a rough awakening when I should actually see the places I had probably glorified in memory. Reality, I had thought, can never catch up with dreams. Now I remembered how I had anticipated this moment: a velvet-thick meadow, a blue sky, sparkling air, a light cool breeze in the sunshine . . .

When I opened my eyes I saw that I had been all wrong. This place was much more beautiful than I had dreamed. It was not just a bucolic painting; it lived, breathed, and was overflowing with the moisture of life. The sounds of grass moving in the wind, of the insects, of the brook were sweet and familiar. I moved over to the brook that came bounding over the rocks, stooped down, and took a long draught of cold water. I sat down on one of the boulders by the bank, dipped my toes in the spray, felt the soil with my hands. The impact of being a visitor in my native land hit me with full force.

I returned to the meadow. Its grass, as I lay down, half buried me. The flowers were at a level with my eyes, some looking down on me. It grew dark as I still lay there, conscious of the moment—conscious and grateful and happy in this hour of fulfillment and pause and unity with the world. In his *Reveries of a Solitary Wanderer* Rousseau said: "Scarcely is there, in our most living delights, a moment where the heart can truly say to us: I wish that this moment should last forever." Goethe must have seen those words, which became the leitmotif of his Faust. I truly felt like yielding to Mephistopheles and "telling time to linger."

Time did linger, forgotten. What did Thomas Wolfe say—"You can't go home again"? You can, Tom, you can.

After three timeless days I rejoined the world.

2. Watershed of History

THE ORIGINAL return trip to the Alps, which took me to the three huts, was to be the first of many more. On the first, fifteen years after I had left the Alps, I was by myself; on some of the others my wife Charlotte and our sons Anthony and Martin were along; and on one I had more than a hundred companions when I introduced my Sierra Club friends to my home mountains.

As I write this, another fifteen years after that first trip, ten pilgrimages to the Alps are behind me, and in my memory they all flow together in a single panorama. I no longer know when it was that I looked down into a valley from this peak or that. The episodes that follow are told in the sequence of that first trip, from east to west, regardless of which year they happened to occur.

Those trips to the Alps have been exercises in self-fulfillment. Man's inner strength spent in daily living and in daily confrontation with his environment is renewed from different sources—satisfactory personal relationships, artistic expressions, religious convictions, creative achievements in professional pursuits. My own renewal comes from visits to my home mountains.

A man's own mountains will never cease to spell home. They are the scene of his first awakening to the wonder of mountains, of experience which could have occurred in any range but which, for him, did occur among his native peaks. The memory of his own mountains does not fade, no matter how distant he may be. Consciously, the traveler will make his hills a standard of reference for all mountains that he sees. Unconsciously, he will find their shadows and their light upon all the mountain ways he ever walks.

The preceding paragraph is cited without quotation marks, in order not to disturb continuity, from an article in the *Sierra Club Bulletin* of June, 1954, "Hills of Home" by Margaret Thal-Larsen. I never met her but she is a sister in spirit, and she said it better than I could. With singular perception she continues, saying that there is one range in which the visitor from afar is likely to feel himself not only "at home" but actually in his own hills. Despite the grip of one's own mountains and the love of native land, says Margaret, the Alps will irresistibly intrude themselves as hills of home upon anyone who comes to know them. She says she has frequently heard visiting European climbers reply to questions from boosters of local peaks. The questions invariably involved a demand

for comparison between the local scene and the Alps. The answer frequently, and with polite ambiguity, was some variant of the reflection that "there are no mountains like the Alps."

Margaret Thal-Larsen asks, of course, why this should be so, and comes to the conclusion that the Alps may claim to be "the other hills of home" to all who love mountains, simply because they are so beautiful and because they have played so large a part in the story and legend of mountaineering.

In Hemingway's "Snows of Kilimanjaro," the hero, facing the snows of the African peak at the moment of his death, remembers the snows of his youth, the snows of Tirol—"as hard as sugar, as dry as powder, so white it hurts the eyes."

If the Alps can become the "home mountains" for those not born there, how much stronger must be the attachment of those for whom they were the home mountains in the first place.

There is a legend in Greek mythology telling how the giant Antaeus wrestled with Hercules. Hercules succeeded in downing the strong giant, but again and again Antaeus rose and continued the fight. Finally Hercules realized that the giant renewed his strength miraculously every time his body touched the soil. His mother was Gaea, the goddess of earth. In the end, Hercules prevailed by lifting Antaeus into the air and strangling him there.

I remember that legend every time I touch the soil of the Alps. My own renewal comes from that touch and, no matter what may have happened before, I feel I can face the demands of life again for a time after my communion with the hills of home.

I have another strong feeling when I am in the Alps, related to Margaret Thal-Larsen's "story and legend of mountaineering," but broader—a feeling not only for the history of mountaineering, but also for the importance of the Alps in the history of Europe and thus of the planet.

The geographic location of the Alps determined their historical role. Their ramparts, cutting a half-moon across the continent from Vienna or Trieste to Genoa, sealed off the Mediterranean, the cradle of Western civilization, from the northern half of Europe. Long after the flowering of Greek and Roman culture, the primitive tribes north of the Alps were still barbarians. One might speculate that had it not been for the protective wall of the Alps, the Romans would have been unable to expand and consolidate their empire and admirable culture; the Germanic tribes could presumably have conquered Rome long before they did—and destroyed Roman civilization, including Christianity. On the other hand, one might speculate further, had there been an extended plain in the heart of the continent, something like the American Midwest, the cultural exchange between the European nations could have softened nationalism, perhaps prevented two world wars, and ultimately have led to the United States of Europe. A few words, then, about the geography of the Alps, before we look at their history.

The Alps stretch 760 miles from west to east or from east to west, depending upon where you start. Since I started in Vienna, I see the Vienna Woods as the "beginning," and therefore the Alps as extending from east to west. But a look at the map shows them as a funnel or cornucopia with the narrow end in the west—the single chain of the Ligurian Alps, widening as you go east into two, then three, finally five ranges; and seen this way, the Alps seem to "begin" in the west.

The Alps cover 80,000 square miles. In oversimplified terms one might say that lengthwise they fall primarily into three roughly parallel chains: the main crystalline "Urgestein" range in the center, and two sedimentary limestone ranges north and south of it. Volcanic cataclysms made the Alps rise up from the sea that originally covered Europe; the sea floor was coated by shell deposits —the sedimentary layer; beneath it was the crystalline rock. After the Alps had been lifted above the sea, some of the sedimentary layer was eroded away to expose the crystalline core below.

Crosswise the Alps are divided into a western and eastern part by a line from Lake Constance to Lake Como across the Splügen pass; or into a western, central, and eastern part, with the Central Alps separated from the Western Alps by the Simplon pass, and from the Eastern Alps by the Reschenscheideck and Stelvio passes. Mont Blanc, 15,782 feet, is the highest summit of the Alps.

Six countries share the Alps—Switzerland, Austria, Italy, France, Germany, Yugoslavia—eight, if you count Liechtenstein and Monaco. Switzerland and Austria have the lion's share; the sections that are now in Italy and Yugoslavia were part of Austria before 1918.

National boundaries, anachronisms everywhere, seem singularly absurd in the integrated system of ranges that is the spine of Europe. Some of the finest peaks thumb their noses on national exclusiveness: Switzerland's Matterhorn is half in Italy, where it is known as Monte Cervino; France's Mont Blanc straddles the Italian border;

the Karawanken range is split lengthwise between Austria and Yugoslavia, the crest forming the border. The highest peak of the old Austrian empire, the Ortler (12,802 feet), became the highest peak of Italy after 1918 and is now called Ortles.

International boundary-drawing reaches the level of burlesque inside Germany's highest mountain, the Zugspitze (9,738 feet). In Germany you climb up (or ride up) one side of the mountain; near the top you enter a horizontal tunnel leading to the opposite side; half-way through, in the bowels of the mountain, you reach an iron gate: the Austrian border. German and Austrian guards check you at each end of the tunnel.

Whenever I return to the Alps I am reminded that I am stepping on historical ground. So many passes are associated with the names of ancient and modern generals who crossed them, so many ruins of medieval castles survive, so many names of places and peaks have Roman roots. Some names, mostly in the Vallais, are said to have Arab roots, reminders of the "Saracens" who made incursions into Switzerland in the tenth century: Pizzo del Moro, Allalin, Almagell; the mountain Mischabel is also mentioned as being a corruption of the Arabic term for "lioness with cubs," although spoilsports say it just means "Mistgabel," dung fork. The name Pontresina may mean "ad pontem Sarasinam," a designation found in a twelfth-century document.

The Alps have been "man's own mountains" since the dawn—and before the dawn—of history. Man is an organic part of the Alps, like the animals and the plants. Man has lived in the Alps for centuries. This is a profoundly important fact and distinguishes the Alps from many, wilder ranges of the world. My awareness of the Alps' being historical started in my childhood when my parents took me during school vacation to Hallstatt in the Salzkammergut lake district. There I was shown the tools and jewels, dated between 1000 and 500 B.C., found at Hallstatt. I remember pictures in the local museum showing the men of the Bronze Age carrying salt from the Hallstatt mine in leather rucksacks and using fire sticks to light up the mines. Copper was also mined in the Salzburgian and Tirolean mountains in the Bronze Age. And I was fascinated to learn that rock engravings found in the Ligurian Alps and in the mountains north of Lake Garda had been dated by archaeologists to the second millenium B.C. The Brenner and Semmering passes were used by man in the Stone Age; and the cave bear was hunted in the Alps even before the last Ice Age ended eight thousand years ago. All these facts were not abstract book stuff to us schoolchildren. The Stone Age Venus of Willendorf, for example, was a statuette that we knew from the museum in Vienna, and the village of Willendorf itself was familiar to us from many Sunday trips along the Danube. (It was a strange sensation for me to see again the buxom, well-coiffed, red-brown 20,000-year-old young lady—half-way around the world and half a century after my first encounter with her—in a museum in San Francisco, where she was a star exhibit in the late sixties, on loan from the Vienna Kunsthistorische Museum.)

Never was I more consciously aware of the historical role of the Alps than the day I crossed a pass where Hannibal supposedly had crossed. The Alps may be said to enter history with Hannibal's celebrated expedition from Spain into Italy in 218 B.C., when he forced his way across somewhere south of Mont Blanc. Since no contemporary accounts exist, historians had a happy time guessing the exact spot. The sources—the Greek writer Polybius (205 to 123 B.C.) and the Roman writer Livy (59 B.C. to A.D. 17)—are vague and disagree. Most writers today say that Hannibal and his Carthaginian army, estimated by Livy at from 20,000 to 100,000 on foot, 6,000 to 20,000 cavalry, and 37 elephants, crossed Montgenèvre in the Cottian Alps, west of Turin. But many other passes have been named as historians interpreted Livy and measured distances, including the Little Saint Bernard, Mont Cenis, the Col de Clapier. Mark Twain once said: "The researches of many antiquarians have already thrown much darkness on the subject, and it is probable, if they continue, that we shall soon know nothing at all."

When I was in high school we were stuffed with Latin for eight years, and Livy was required reading. One of the few passages that caught our fancy was Livy's account of Hannibal's trip—how "the bearded men" in the Alps attacked his army from behind the precipices—and, of course, the historian's comments on the elephants. A sixteenth-century English translator of the passage, Philemon Holland, wrote: "The poor elephants were ever readie and anone to run upon their noses, and the snow being once with the gate of so many people and beasts upon it fretted and thawed, they were fain to go upon the bare yce underneeth and in the slabberie snow-broth as it relented and melted about their heeles." The picture of the elephants running on their noses was evocative for me, even then, of the "Nosobame"—an animal that walks on its many noses—a grotesque creation of the German poet Christian Morgenstern. Standing at that pass as a high-school student, and with Livy on my mind, I caught myself hunting for elephant tracks among the automobile tire markings on the ground.

Hannibal, according to Livy-Holland, had a hard time; big boulders hindered his progress, but he "powred theron strong vinegar to calcine and dissolve it"—a method unfamiliar to mountain scramblers today. But he made it. It took him fifteen days to cross into Italy, and then fifteen years to hound the Romans—but with less success. The Roman general, Scipio, carried the war into Hannibal's homeland and defeated him in North Africa.

We high-school boys from Vienna, living close to the Alps, also learned (in Latin and history classes) what happened in the Alps after Hannibal: the Romans under Caesar and Augustus subjugated the tribes on the north side of the divide, and erected monuments, still existing, to commemorate the accomplishments—a triumphal arch at Susa, near Turin, and a tower at La Turbie, on the French Riviera. The Alps became a Roman chain. Charlemagne, moving in the opposite direction, drove his men south across the Alps, conquered the Lombards in upper Italy in A.D. 774, and in successive operations combined, for the second and last time in history, the whole range under the rule of one man.

The testimonies of man living in the Alps throughout the Middle Ages are castles and fortresses, some in ruins, others inhabited to this day, which dominate hundreds of picturesque high spots in the Alpine valleys. Excursions to these places were among the highlights of our high-school history classes; with scientific thoroughness we inspected the savage torture instruments and brutal butchering weapons in the armories; in the castle of Hohensalzburg there is a "sweatbox," actually a stove, into which human beings were stuffed in a crouching position, and roasted alive. And we took note, with stomach-fluttering awe, of the nozzles through which boiling pitch was poured onto the enemy trying to scale the walls. I remember one castle in Tirol whose top floor could be tilted on hinges in such a way that the besieged knights could slide into freedom over the heads of their enemies, escaping on the seats of their pants. Many of these fortified castles were the core of the towns and villages that developed around them, as the place names ending in "-burg" indicate to this day.

We learned about the medieval and modern rulers who crossed the Alps. One was the crusader, Frederick Barbarossa, in 1162. Another was Napoleon. Fascinated by Hannibal's exploit in attacking the enemy from the rear, Napoleon crossed the Great Saint Bernard pass in May 1800 with 34,000 men on his way from Dijon to Italy, to defeat the Austrians near the village of Marengo. The barrels of his cannon were dragged across "in hollowed-out tree trunks," as we were told, although we could not visualize this very well; and the wheels were stuck on poles and carried by Napoleon's army. I was impressed by a Jacques-Louis David oil painting of Napoleon I once saw in Versailles, showing the emperor idealized as he crossed the Alpine pass on a white charger—although in fact he plodded along on a mule. We were told that when he reached the famed hospice of Saint Bernard, he asked the canons for a copy of Livy, in order to read up on Hannibal; and that he wrung out his hat that had been soaked by rain—but the painting did not show this soggy episode. Hannibal's Alpine crossing occupied Napoleon's mind even in exile; writing in Saint Helena he speculated, like so many after him, about the route taken by the ancient general.

The Alps were battlegrounds in both world wars. In the First World War the Austrians and Italians faced each other in the Dolomites, with fierce battles raging high above the clouds. Both sides were entrenched in the rugged peaks, exchanging artillery fire across the glaciers and precipices. The troops reached these fantastic positions by exposed trails and tramways. One summer, in my high-school days, when I was climbing in the Dolomites, an Austrian guide gave me a pair of binoculars and had me look at a flattish mountain top, which did not seem particularly remarkable to me—until he explained that that top had not always been flat. On one dramatic occasion in the First World War, Austrian artillery blew off the entire top of that mountain, Col di Lana, where the Italians had been entrenched in summit caverns. I was unable to share in the patriotic enthusiasm of the guide over the feat of Austrian warriors. Ski troops were also used at that time, among them the champion Luis Trenker who later starred in a movie portraying the episode.

In the Second World War, French *Chasseurs Alpins* faced Italian *Alpini* and, later, Nazi *Gebirgsjäger* in the Mont Blanc region. French mountain troops near Chamonix were the last to give up in 1940, and by August 1944, as part of the Résistance, had recovered the French Alps in Haute Savoie a year before the final German defeat. Among them was the famed climber Lionel Terray. In the intervening years, 1943 and 1944, the Alps served as precarious escape routes for French and British soldiers held prisoners in Italian camps; according to Claire Engel, *A History of Mountaineering in the Alps*, 1,600 made it into Switzerland through passes at the top of the Viège valleys, 1,500 in the Simplon region; the total number of refugees is unknown.

The conduct of the Second World War, to an important degree, was masterminded from the Alps. There, in an incredible eyrie at the top of 5,700-foot Kehlstein above Berchtesgaden, accessible only through a 400-foot

tunnel drilled through solid rock, the German warlord made his decisions contemplating the view from his summer chancellery, the "Eagle's Nest."

I had an odd sensation as I rode up the Kehlstein in the lavish bronze elevator, decorated in red, in which only he and some of his select ever traveled. The ride ended at a fortresslike terrace, facing a stunning Wagnerian panorama of the Bavarian and Austrian Alps. I stepped onto one of the low stone enclosures. It was from this very spot that Herr Supreme Commander hatched his enormities. And now I owned the place. Literally! The Eagle's Nest today is a restaurant owned by the Alpine Club, whose membership card I, the returned refugee, carried in my pocket. If there is such an emotion as "humble triumph" —this was what I felt.

Our age of technology has made the Alps "man's own mountains" more than ever. Man has changed the barrier of the Alps into a chain between north and south. A marker at one of the Alpine passes says *Aquas disiungo, populos iungo* —I separate the oceans, I unite the people. There is painful ambivalence in man's attitude as he invades the solitude of the Alps. He seems sorry and proud at the same time as he builds his highways, bridges, and tunnels; he is guilt-ridden as he attempts to make his technical accomplishments themselves beautiful or impressive, and to design them in such a way as to bring out the natural beauty of the mountains. The road over the Stelvio pass, the Grossglockner road, the Silvretta road, the Col d'Iseran road are more than engineering feats; they are constructed to give the visitor a grandiose panorama of the surrounding mountains, as if to apologize that they are, at the same time, violating the wildness.

The most recent accomplishments, if that is the correct word, are the Europa Bridge and the Mont Blanc tunnel. The Europa Bridge, completed in 1963, rises 623 feet from the Sill River valley south of Innsbruck. The highest span in Europe, the highest pillar-supported bridge in the world, it fits gracefully into the scenery as it relieves the formerly tortuous access to the Brenner pass.

The Mont Blanc tunnel, completed in 1964, connects the Haute Savoie region of France with the Aosta valley of Italy, for the most direct route between Paris and Rome; it is the world's longest automobile tunnel, a seven-mile tube, piercing Mont Blanc.

For better or worse, the Alps, the barrier of Antiquity that cut Europe in two, have become the highway between the northern and southern part of the continent: *populos iungo*. From the burrows in the Bronze Age to the tunnel through Mont Blanc, the Alps remain man's own mountains.

Interlude

THE AWAKENING

In 1937 The Grabhorn Press, through the good work of J. Monroe Thorington, W. Dock, and Francis P. Farquhar, published Conrad Gesner: On the Admiration of Mountains. *In a prefatory note Mr. Dock wrote: "In the second decade of the sixteenth century the Alps for the first time were described and depicted as a playground, an ideal one for the nobles who hunted the chamois. During the next twenty years the natural philosophers who gave such lustre to Swiss science discovered that enquiring and appreciative minds were stimulated by traveling through mountain forests and meadows, by climbing toward the lofty peaks. This novel idea, evidence of a revolution in human thought, found its most vigorous statement in two essays by Conrad Gesner."*

Mr. Thorington's biographical sketch fills in the context: "The boy, Gesner [b. 1516], came into a word of amazing change. . . . Leonardo da Vinci, father of experimental science, was still living, an old man in a new world, while Copernicus was not yet ready to publish his dangerously novel theory of the earth and planets wheeling around the sun. The voices which stirred the land were those of Luther and Calvin. . . . Gesner's interests were diverse and profound. His Universal Dictionary, *published when he was twenty-seven, contained summaries of all the known books in Hebrew, Greek, Latin, French and German . . . and he was probably the first to point out that plants must be classified according to the structure of flowers and fruit. . . . Death, coming to him with the plague of 1565, . . . ended a life devoted to learning, to his family, and to the enjoyment of the mountains.*

"But Gesner's . . . actual attainments as a mountaineer, and his projected work on the Alps interest us less than Gesner the man, walking joyful and unafraid in the mountains, delighting in rustic pleasure. . . . It is thus that he takes his place among the greatest of the early mountaineers, the eloquent exponent of a new and intrepid devotion to high country. . . . One is certain that he would find a welcome place in any company of modern climbers."

And in the company of modern Renaissance men, of whom there need be more.

D.R.B.

I say therefore that he is an enemy of nature, whosoever has not deemed lofty mountains to be worthy of great contemplation. Surely the height of the more elevated mountains seems already to have risen above a baser lot and to have escaped from our storms, as though lying within another world. There the force of the most powerful sun, of the air and of the winds is not the same. The snows linger perpetually, the softest of objects, which melts even at the touch of the fingers, recks not at all for any glow or violence of the sun's heat: nor banishes with time but rather freezes into the most enduring ice and everlasting crystal. . . . Who might properly reckon the varieties of animals and the fodder of wild beasts aloft in the mountains? Whatever in other places nature offers here and there but sparingly, in the mountains she presents everywhere and in sufficiency as though in a heap so to speak, she spreads it out, unfolds it, and sets before the eye all her treasure, all her jewels. And so all of the elements and the variety of nature the supreme wonder resides in the mountains. In these it is possible to see "the burden of the mighty earth," just as if nature were vaunting herself & making trial of her strength, by lifting to such a height so great a weight, which still of its own accord and by reason of the most heavy pressure is every ready to slip downward.

Which indeed of the senses does not enjoy its own proper pleasure? For to consider the matter of *feeling*, the whole body, troubled by heat, is singularly refreshed on meeting with the cooler air prevailing in the mountains, which from every quarter blows upon the surface of the body and is breathed in to our full capacity; this is in accord with the well-known line of Homer: "He revived when the cold breath of Boreas blew upon him." On the other hand, the same body, having experienced wind and cold, is warmed by the sun, by walking, or by a fire in the huts of the herdsmen.

Sight is charmed by the wondrous and unwonted appearance of mountains, ridges, rocks, forests, valleys, streams, springs and meadows. As for color, for the most part everything is fresh and blooming; as to the form of the things which are seen, strange and unusual are the aspects of crags, rocks, winding ways and other things, worthy of admiration not only for their form but also for their size and height. If you wish to extend your field of vision, cast your glance round about, and gaze off far and wide at everything. There is no lack of lookouts and crags on which you may seem to yourself to be already living with your head in the clouds. If on the other hand you should prefer to contract your vision, you will gaze on meadows and verdant forests, or even enter them; or to narrow it still more, you will examine dim valleys, shadowy rocks and darksome caverns. Moreover, while there is change and variety in all these things, it is most delightful of all in those perceived by the senses. In truth, nowhere else is such great variety found within such small compass as in the mountains; in which, not to speak of other things, one may in a single day behold & enter upon the four seasons of the year, summer, autumn, spring and winter. In addition, from the highest ridges of mountains the whole dome of our sky will lie boldly open to your gaze, and the rising and setting of the constellations you will easily behold without any hindrance; while you will observe the sun setting far later and likewise rising earlier.

. . .

As for *hearing*, it will be diverted by the conversation, jests and witticisms of friends, as well as by the exceeding sweet songs of the little birds in the woods, and finally by the very silence of the solitude. There is nothing here to be offensive to the ears, nothing to be troublesome, no uproar or noise of the cities, no strife of mankind. Here amid the deep and, as it were, religious hush, from the lofty ridges of the mountains you will seem to perceive the actual harmony, if such there be, of the celestial spheres.

Likewise pleasing *odors* from herbs, flowers & shrubs of the mountains present themselves. For the same plants grow in the mountains as in the plain, only in the former more fragrant and more efficacious as remedies. The air here is far more free and healthful, and not corrupted by gross exhalations to the same degree as on level ground, not contagious or foul as in cities and other dwelling places of men. This air distributed by the nostrils to the brain, and by the arteries to the lungs and heart, not only is harmful but is even soothing to them.

I have already above sung the praises of that exceptional delight to the *taste*, a drink of cold water. This indeed will afford joy to the weary and thirsty with no injury at all, or with much less than would be the case in the plain. For in the first place, the water itself in the mountains is purer and better, especially about half way up, unless I mistake: at this point it is not too cold or like snow, and yet it is pure and filtered and still exposed to the open air; while about the summits either there is none, or else it is excessively cold and glacial and not sufficiently pure or filtered.

. . .

Let us then conclude that from walks in the mountains undertaken in the company of friends the highest of all pleasures and the most charming of all delights of the senses are obtained, provided there be no hindrance in the weather, and none in either mind or body. For to a man who is sick or unsound of limb nothing of this sort can be welcome. So also if his mind be ill, if he have not laid aside anxieties and passions, in vain are the pleasures of body and senses sought for. But give me a man at least moderately endowed in mind and body, educated liberally, and not too much given to idleness and luxury or to lust; also I should wish him curious about natural objects and an admirer of them, so that even from the contemplation and admiration of the mighty works of the Supreme Architect & of the enormous variety of nature as it exhibits itself in the mountains, as though in a single vast pile, the delight of his spirit might be added to the harmonious delight of all his senses; what other sort of pleasure will you find, pray, at least within the bounds of nature, more honorable, more complete, and more perfect from every point of view? But walking itself and fatigue are tiresome and tedious. There is also danger in the difficulties of the region and in the steep places. The allurements of food and bed are lacking. Grant that these things are true; it will be pleasant thereafter to recall the toils and the dangers; it will gratify you to turn over these things in your mind and to tell them to friends. Actually the very pleasure derived from repose following upon toil is destined to be so much the greater, and health even more rugged, in a man such as I require, with at least an ordinary constitution. For all the parts of the body are exercised in a man walking, and sometimes leaping; all the sinews and muscles stretch and toil, some in the ascent, others in the descent; and in a different way in each of these cases, according as the direction is straight ahead or slanting, as happens in the mountains. But it is possible and advisable to employ a certain moderation in walking; and it is a fact, as Aristotle writes in his *Problemata*, "that people walking over uneven places become less exhausted than they would on the level." That is to say, those who by turn ascend and descend, as is the nature of mountain journeys, are less fatigued than those who journey either for a long time across a plain, or only up or only down.

. . .

It is possible also for the dangers of rocks and of other sorts to be avoided by those who have come to understand either that they are subject to giddiness or are otherwise unfitted for overcoming steep places. It is something to have got so far, if farther is not granted. As for foods, I have told above and will tell again later what ones and what quality are found in the mountains, which assuredly will satisfy even fastidious men; especially since it is necessary for them to abstain for one or two days from their customary food. And those dairy products, although unusual, still work no harm at all to most walkers, because of the exercise.
So that men fond of their palate, if only for this reason ought now and then to visit the mountains, that they might have a chance to drink cold water and enjoy milk and the various foods and delicacies made from it without injury to stomach and health; a thing which it is not permitted most at home, even if these things were at hand and of equal excellence.
If, however, other foods were absolutely required, they can easily be brought by servants.

But couch, mattress, feather bed and pillows are lacking. O, soft and effeminate man! For you, hay will take the place of all these; it is soft, fragrant, composed of various herbs and the most health-giving flowers; your breathing at night will prove far more pleasant and wholesome. This you may spread beneath your head for a pillow, beneath your whole body for a mattress; and you may also spread it over you for a coverlet.

But I return to the geography of the mountain. In the highest cowherd's hut, after we had been refreshed with the richest and most delicious milk and had blown the alpine horn (of a length of about eleven feet, formed of two pieces of wood slightly bent and hollowed out, and cleverly bound together by withes), thence we turned to the left led by a milker from that hut. And presently becoming three-footed, that is to say leaning upon staves, to which they give the name "alpenstocks" and which they are wont to provide with an iron point, we climbed a long way without a path up an exceeding steep slope; at times we even: crept along by taking hold of the clumps of grass; and among rocks and stones, with great toil, at length we came out on top.

Tiefkarspitze and western Karwendelspitze, Germany

Sonnenspitze, Wampeter Schrofen, Marienbergspitze, near Fern pass, Austria

GUIDO REY

Peaks and Precipices: Scrambles in the Dolomites and Savoy *is the work from which the following excerpts, translated from the Italian by J. E. C. Eaton, have been taken, and is almost a history of Guido Rey's Alpine career. Eaton speaks highly of Rey's intense love of the mountains, his climbing skills, and poetic thoughts, his modesty, and his humor, and in the last two traces a resemblance to Mummery. The book, Rey's last, was published in 1914. ". . . if climbers remained as good and as pure in the plains," Rey wrote, "as they were in their ideal moments on the summit, other men, seeing them return, would believe them to be a troop of angels descended from heaven. But climbers, when they go home, become once more prey to their weaknesses, resume their bad habits, and write their articles for Alpine Journals!" But they can also write wonderful books, like Rey's* Peaks and Precipices *and his* The Matterhorn.

D.R.B.

A hymn of gratitude was welling from my heart, which was at peace and no longer mistrustful of those mysterious shapes.

One single day had sufficed to slake a curiosity that I had nurtured for years, and my Alpine career, now nearing its close, was enriched with a new beauty.

This thought alone stood out clearly in my mind during that first period of repose, after the great excitement my senses had undergone; my muscles were still shaking with the efforts they had put forth; as I lay motionless on a rock I still had a feeling of continued motion, as when one disembarks after a stormy passage. And yet I discovered within me an exceptional mental balance, a security, a strange keenness in all my faculties, as if the contest had awakened hitherto unsuspected powers in me. I enjoyed the repose like a healthy animal that comes weary but victorious out of a fight, sure of its strength and its cunning and ready to fight again.

It may be that this suddenly revived consciousness of inherited instinctive faculties is one of the deepest and most acceptable self-revelations which we attain through the savage struggle with the mountains, and it is each time a cause of surprise, and almost a shock to us, as if a being new and unknown had made his appearance in us, and for the time replaced that other individual, full of weaknesses and pride, who is wont to walk in our likeness during our daily life in cities.

. . .

It seems as if the modern, civilized man, sated with artificialities and luxury, were wont, when he returns to the primeval mountains, to find among their caves his prehistoric brother, alive and unchanged, a simple child of Nature, whose foot is sure and whose eye is accustomed to wide spaces; he seems to recognize with a joy a survivor of his family's early unrecorded struggles with untamed Nature, to unite with him, and to let himself be led through the terrible visions of a prehistoric landscape, to renew for a day the ancient war which tempered the human race in its infancy.

. . .

From Nebelhorn toward Mädelegabel and Höfats, Bavaria

I recalled to memory the many bivouacs that had fallen to my lot during my wanderings in the Alps, from the Ecrins to the Weisshorn, from the Meije to Monte Rosa, from the Grivola to the Punta Bianca, from Monte Viso to the Furggen ride of the Matterhorn. . . .

And always, in joyous bivouacs as in sad ones, on those which preceded victory as in those which followed defeat, there was always the same fascination that I now experienced once more —a secret thrill, a sense of wonder, an expectation of something indefinable, something mysterious, that was about to become manifest.

Now that the agony of my long and sustained effort had ceased, I began to hear a confused murmur of voices and of sounds that came from every side, rising from the valleys and falling from the summit; starting from afar, it increased in intensity as it drew nearer, and then rolled swiftly away in the distance. It was the like the sighs of spirits flying above my head. Amid the low yet powerful sounds of the huge chorus I could sometimes distinguish a sharper note, as of anger or lamentation, which soon ceased, while another voice was uplifted in answer from afar.

This was the high dialogue between the mountains and the sky, but on that night all the voices, great and small, seemed to seek out the tiny mortal who lay lonely and abandoned on the mountain's bosom, and to relate to him a long and wonderful tale, as ancient as the world itself.

. . .

Pordoi in Sella massif, Dolomites

That which once appeared as simply an amusement for my idle hours and an outlet for the superabundant energy of youth, has now become a strict element in the regulation of my life and a necessary support for my declining strengths; in my heart, which is now closed to the ingenuous conceits of my early years, insensible to the rivalries which incited me of yore to deeds of daring, careless of the applause which it formerly prized as the guerdon of victory, there is now but one pure flame, that burns gently and steadily, and does not flicker with the breath of praise or blame. I know that were I to return to the place whence I started, I should again choose without hesitation the road to the mountains.

But life's span is short; the fatal year is close at hand when the approach of the summer will no longer be a signal for the secret and anxious consideration of bold and cherished plans, for preparations hidden from all, and for the usual departure towards the unknown. Rope and sack and axe will remain hanging on the wall like trophies of ancient arms. I shall no longer return from my mysterious absences with garments torn and hands peeled, nor shall I come proudly home with my face all burned by the Alpine sun.

. . .

And from the sparkling slopes, from the immense fields of snow, from the pure white peaks, the memories of past hours will descend to me in slow procession, and each one will awaken an interest in me, and will look upon me with a familiar glance and tell me its name.

GUIDO REY (*c. 1900*)

Monte Cervino, from Lago Bleu, Italy

3. Fritzi

MY VISITS to the Alps, after that first return trip, mostly started in the Vienna Woods. These woodlands have been overadvertised, sugarized, and strausswaltzed, and inevitably fall short of expectations when visitors to Vienna spend an afternoon in them—usually driving up the Kahlenberg automobile road. The view is pleasant enough from the Kahlenberg restaurant, and the visitors will politely praise the scenery.

But the tales of the Vienna Woods were born before the automobile roads and tourist restaurants were built, and to understand the magic of these woods one has to take the trouble to follow the trails. They are not wilderness trails, because they usually lead to a village or a "Jausenstation" (an inn where you can get a drink or a snack), and you are likely to meet people. But they lead past or through charming meadows and woods, and their spell is unbroken only a stone's throw from the road. The characteristic tree in the Vienna Woods is the beech—light, graceful, lacy, the branches and trunks playing in the wind in all directions. I took a photograph of them and found it in stunning contrast to another photograph I took of a forest in Tirol near Krimml, where the firm, straight trunks of firs formed a phalanx like soldiers; I think of the Vienna Woods beeches as "the women's forest" and of the Tirolean firs as "the men's forest."

The Sunday outing into the Vienna Woods—the "Ausflug"—was, and still is, a way of life to the Viennese. My father, from whom I inherited my love of the mountains, would look out the window early on Sunday mornings to appraise the weather—forecasts were not so well developed in those days, and outings had to be based on hunches. If he diagnosed the situation as safe, friends were mobilized by telephone to meet at one of Vienna's trolley terminals—Sievering, Grinzing, Pötzleinsdorf—to be reached within a half hour from downtown. These terminals were the roadheads of the trails that led into the Vienna Woods, extensions of the foothills of the Alps. Nobody who was anybody among us hikers owned an automobile—that was a privilege of the rich or of foreigners, and treated with disdain by us who loved the trails. In later years, when I returned to my California home from an outing in the Sierra Nevada, I often regretted that the companionship always ended when we each reached our automobiles parked at the pack stations. We would then drive home for many hours, each locked in his own mobile cell. Our Alpine outings did not end when we reached the trolley terminals. We would all climb in and ride home together, savoring and discussing our joint experience, sometimes singing on the way back.

It was here, in the Vienna Woods, that our son Anthony, then ten, had his day in one of the frillier episodes of my Alpine wanderings—and thereby hangs a major tale.

Anthony was thrilled by the green, grassy expanse spread before him from one of the hills. "Wall-to-wall meadow," he said. But later his attention was arrested by something else: between the village of Salmannsdorf and the popular woodsy outdoor inn known as Hameau, he spotted a snake, three feet long. When he grabbed it, it whipped around and bit him. Anthony screamed—not from pain but because he had let go. "Grab him, Daddy, quickly, before he escapes."

If I had only known what I was getting myself into when, induced by the urgency of his request, I chased the snake! I managed to pin it down in the middle, but its head shot out like a jet plane, and it bit me too. I now seized it behind the head, while the rest wound itself around my arm. Anthony heaved a sigh of relief. The snake was ours.

Two small drops of blood seeped from his finger and mine. We did not know what kind of snake we had caught. We decided to take it to the Hameau inn, hoping that someone there would identify it. "If he's poisonous," Anthony said, "at least we'll know what we died of."

The Hameau inn was full of snake experts, but they disagreed with each other. Still, they all said that the snake was not poisonous. As one of them summed up: Rattlesnakes do not exist in the Alps, and if it were a "Kreuzotter" (a common adder, the only poisonous Alpine snake), I would not have been so foolish as to have myself bitten without rushing to see a doctor.

On our way to the trolley that was to take us back to the city I tried to persuade Anthony to let the snake go— our hostess, Frau Minna Donner, would not appreciate it. Have you ever tried to persuade a ten-year-old to give up a pet snake? Exactly.

Did Frau Donner scream when she opened the door and saw the snake? Frau Donner has two boys herself. She cut short Anthony's prepared speech. "There's a shoebox in the bathroom," she said with a wry smile.

Days went by, and weeks. Anthony found a picture of Fritzi in the encyclopedia—it was a harmless aesculap, symbol of the peaceful medical profession. Our wounds had healed, Fritzi had eaten a mouse that Anthony had purchased in a pet store, and now was satisfied for an indefinite period. Fritzi, by now, lived in a luxurious terrarium, unconcerned with the future.

But Anthony pondered the future and our pending return to the distant shores of America. Waiting for a psychologically felicitous moment, he aired the question of the snake's immigration to the United States.

"You're crazy, Tony," I said with conviction. "There are undoubtedly a dozen regulations against this—a veterinarian's certificate, quarantine, inoculation, what do I know. We won't even discuss it. The snake, of course, stays here."

Why "of course"? Couldn't I inquire from the Customs Department of the U.S. Consulate in Vienna . . . ?

"Sorry," said the Customs man, "we don't know about snakes. If you really want to pursue this, you'd have to get in touch with the Consulate at Frankfurt am Main in Germany." I gritted my teeth and wrote to Frankfurt.

The answer came promptly, with Yankee efficiency: "Sir, concerning your inquiry we wish to inform you that the importation of a live snake is not against any federal law, provided you can produce a certificate of the U.S. Consulate in Vienna confirming that the export of the reptile does not violate Austrian law."

"We got this far, Daddy," said Anthony satisfied. "Now the certificate."

There must have been an edge in my voice when I asked the Vienna Consulate over the telephone why they did not say so in the first place. Who has jurisdiction in snake matters—Vienna or Frankfurt?

Shortly after, I received a letter on official stationery ("The Foreign Office of the United States of America") informing us that, after consultation with the Office of the Veterinary of the City of Vienna, it had been determined: There was no objection to the export of aesculaps, and this letter could be presented to the customs official at the port of arrival in the United States.

Armed with the letter, and with a wooden box specially made for the occasion and ventilated by air holes, we were ready for landing at the airport in New York. Anthony had given fresh water to Fritzi at short stops in Shannon and Gander and had determined that he was not airsick and was evidently content curled up among his leaves.

But just before landing, Anthony felt uneasy. Would the customs people pay any attention to the certificate? Perhaps there were some local regulations after all—you cannot carry even an apple over the California border, for example. Did the officials in Vienna know everything? He took his Alpine import from the box and slipped the snake inside his shirt. But Fritzi, instead of obligingly straightening out, rolled himself into a ball that clearly protruded above Anthony's belt—a customs man would have to be blind not to see it.

The plane rolled to a halt, and we had no more time. I grabbed Fritzi, stuffed him into a plastic bag with a pull string, which previously had housed my toothbrush and shaving cream, and stuffed the bag plus contents in the pocket of my Alpine loden coat.

Anybody who has gone through the New York customs in summer knows how long it takes and how chokingly hot it is. I was sorry for Fritzi, and afraid he would suffocate. Charitably I slipped my hand in my pocket and loosened the string . . .

The customs man noticed nothing. The ordeal over, I slumped down on a suitcase ten feet away from the man, breathing relief. It was at this moment that, like Venus from the waves, Fritzi rose from my coat collar, standing up vertically as if he wanted to give the customs man an especially good view of himself.

Laocoön never wrestled as fiercely with his snake as I did when I grabbed the refugee, pulled him out, and pushed him into a hurridly unzipped suitcase—it was too cumbersome to relocate him in his wooden box.

Customs men in New York are busy people. No one had observed the incident. Fritzi and we arrived safely in California. I had done my fatherly duty and brought home our guest from the Vienna Woods—I did not wish to break a boy's heart.

Immediately after arrival at home, Anthony disappeared next door to see his pal Victor. When he returned, five minutes later, he sported a new wrist watch. "Where did this come from?" I asked. "From Victor. Swapped it for Fritzi. It has a red dial."

4. The Most Enduring Ice

FOR WEEKS you can roam the trails of the Vienna Woods without duplicating your steps. Running southwest from the course of the Danube, the Vienna Woods melt into the chains of Lower Austria and Styria, reaching 7,000 feet in the Hochschwab. Following the mountains farther westward you reach the Salzkammergut, the fair lake area between the Enns and Danube rivers. The region is divided among the lands of Upper Austria, Styria, and Salzburg; at the point where the three come together rises 9,830-foot Dachstein, highest mountain in eastern Austria, peak of the poets, immortalized in song and verse.

The Dachstein ("Rocky Roof"), with the pride of a king wearing his coronation robe, carries the first (that is, easternmost) glaciers of the Alps. When I was a child, this mountain was my first encounter with the ice world of the Alps. When I saw it again on one of the later occasions, I recalled all my glacier trips in the intervening years.

Today two cableways lead easily to the glacier that earlier had been accessible only to those who had worked their way up the mountain. When I revisited the Dachstein, I spent two days at the mountain, on the first day taking the cableway from the lake-area town of Obertraun in the north, on the second, from the Enns-valley town of Schladming.

The cableway on the north goes to a plateau from which you can see the main glacier in all its power; that on the south takes you onto the glacier itself—you open the cabin door and step onto the ice.

Going up on the north side, I interrupted the ride to take a look at the Dachstein ice caves and their bizarre icicle formations; light effects were installed, not in color and on the whole inoffensive.

The cableway continued to the top station, Krippenstein, and I fled from the crowd. In the Alps you can easily get away from the population explosion even in the popular places. Five minutes away from the station I bedded myself, in golden solitude, on the moss patches enclosed by low-growing dwarf firs, the "Latschen" that grow at these altitudes. Spread before me, profiled against the tinted sky, was the enormous glacier, framed by the classical outlines of the Dachstein peaks, so familiar from earlier encounters when I had observed them from the picture-book villages of Gosau or Altaussee. Watching the primeval scene was like watching the expanse of the ocean—the horizon encompassing an infinite world.

The view from the south, the next day, was different. The cableway shooting steeply up climbs the wall to a top station that sits precariously on a crag from which the glacier extends. It must have been a triumph for the architect of this bold venture to put the finishing touches on the audaciously perched structure.

I stepped onto the station platform, and the view dramatically changed from the barren rock I had seen in the cableway cabin as it ascended the wall before me. Now the dark rocks switched to the white gold of the ice lying in the sun as the car reached the top. The first thing I saw was a skier flashing down the glacier—this in midsummer. The ice felt strange underfoot as I stepped from the cabin, but a thin layer of snow provided a firm step. No mosses here to settle in, as on the north side. The icefield was interrupted only by a few boulders and by the peaks whose outline I had seen yesterday.

I sat down on one of the boulders. I picked up a loose, solid piece of clear ice, held it against the sun, and stared into the beautiful crystal reflecting the sun's rays from its planes and edges.

How many years since we skied down the Rothmoos glacier in Tirol, "topless" in the warm winter sun (but nursing our sunburns in the evening)? There had been no

Bernina massif: Piz Glüschaint and Rosegg glacier toward M. Disgrazia, Switzerland

crevasses in that glacier where we skied, and what jubilant freedom as we flew down into the valley. . . . How different had the Rhone glacier been, that jagged maze of pinnacles and spires and serrated chasms, and how blue it was! A tunnel was carved into it, with sides like turquoise glass, eerie and incredible. . . . And the tongue of the upper Grindelwald glacier was the same deep, turquoise blue, and the tip had an opening, a mysterious indigo grotto, like the entrance to another world. . . . What a sight, from the Jungfraujoch, of Europe's largest glacier: glittering Aletschgletscher, fifteen miles long, two miles wide, 1,600 feet thick, unfolding its ermine flawlessness . . . Also, the glaciers of the Dolomites—the fortress of the Marmolata, the threat of Ortler, the imperiousness of Adamello . . . The sovereign ice mantles of Piz Palü, Bernina, Morteratsch . . .

The light refractions of the crystal scintillated in the sun. There are thousands of glaciers in the Alps—three hundred of them more than four miles long. And all these behemoths move! At a rate of thirty to six hundred feet per year—and in Greenland, they say, glaciers can move one hundred feet per *day!*

But in recent years many glaciers (almost all in Switzerland) have regressed—the Morteratsch at the rate of fifty feet per year. Even in my own time, between two visits thirty years apart, I had seen, from the Berliner hut, the strange difference of the Waxegg glacier in the Ziller valley Alps—an ice cataract before, and a dry rocky trough in its lower part, later.

I remembered reading that all glaciers of the earth combined, not counting those near the poles, make up only 3 percent of the total. All others are in Antarctica and Greenland; if these should melt through a rise in the earth's temperature, the oceans would rise two or three hundred feet and disastrously flood the earth. The gla-

ciers, also, command the greatest erosive power in existence and shaped our continents in the Ice Age. Something of the tough persistence of the glaciers in smoothing the rough environment seemed to me reflected in the hardy herdsmen who wrest their livelihood from the mountains.

A strange snorting noise came from the sky—a helicopter circled above, wholly unexpected in this scene. A few feet away, it deftly settled down on the ice. Then it took off—the pilot was practicing—only to sit down again, a few moments later, like a mosquito, on one of the boulders, which was scarcely larger than the craft itself. Helicopters are now widely used in the Alps for rescue operations and to supply some of the larger club huts.

The last Ice Age ended only eight thousand years ago, and it is said that we probably now live in an interglacial period. To think that man of the following age may find helicopters encased in the ice, the way we find mammoths . . .

I found myself wishing that the glaciers could be let alone and not buzzed with helicopters and cableways. As I walked back slowly I passed a marker telling about the terrible fate of a flock of ill-equipped youngsters on a school excursion on the glacier some years ago: A storm came up and buried them in the greatest tragedy of the Dachstein. And yet, I could not help thinking, may the glaciers never be tamed to the point where schoolchildren insufficiently prepared and supervised could unwisely challenge them. The words of the pioneer Alpinists are still true: There is no mountain in the Alps that may not be climbed with perfect safety by practiced mountaineers with good guides, in fine weather, and under favorable snow conditions, and there is no mountain in the Alps that may not become dangerous if the climbers are inexperienced, the guides incompetent, the weather bad, and the snow unfavorable.

5. Hinterlingen

IF YOU WISH to see the highest peak of the Alps, there is no question of which it is. The most beautiful peak, or the most beautiful view of the Alps, is more difficult to name. Many give the prize to the view from the Gornergrat of the Matterhorn and its satellites of the Alps' arctic world; others to the view of the Jungfrau from Wengernalp, of the Wetterhorn from Rosenlaui, of the Eiger-Mönch-Jungfrau from the Schynige Platte, and of the Mischabel horns from Saas-Fee. But if you did not want to see this or that mountain, but "the Alps"—if you had just one day and wanted an over-all impression, a sight characteristic of that great chain, where would you go?

If you ask people you will get a different answer every time. What is "characteristic" of the Alps? In what way are they different from other mountain systems of the world?

No single feature is unique to the Alps. Other mountains have glaciers and striking formations and challenging walls. What distinguishes the Alps, I believe, is the combination of alps, glaciers, and man—the specific carpet-like variety of Alpine mountain pastures, the dramatic icescapes, and the fact that man is an integral part of these mountains.

Where, then, can you see "the Alps"? My own choice is the Hafelekar peak, 7,000 feet, directly north of Innsbruck. On a clear day, looking south, you can see an unbroken row from the Stubai-valley chain, with its spectacular Zuckerhütl pyramid on your far right, to the regal Grossglockner, "the Great Bell Ringer," Austria's highest mountain, at 12,461 feet; the Glockner is just a man's height short of being a "Viertausender," one of the select club of 4,000-meter peaks of which Switzerland is so proud.

Old Toni Schlechtleitner sits on top of Hafelekar with a telescope; for a dime he will let you look through. Year in, year out he is up there; his hair has turned to ash and his skin to leather. He insists that you can see the Dachstein. A peek through the telescope is a good buy, because then you are also eligible to get answers to questions. Toni won't talk to you otherwise. He knows each one of the points, their altitude, and their distance from Hafelekar; he will tell you about them in his heavy Tirolean German, and he will also show you chamois through his glass. Don't talk back to him; he knows what he knows, and he doesn't care to argue. His glass is strong enough to show the snowtracks of a party that climbed the Zuckerhütl that morning, thirty miles away.

Once, after arriving in Innsbruck from California, I took the first cableway up the Hafelekar without even unpacking my suitcase. For the first time, after a long period, I heard German again, as I found myself the only "foreigner" among a group of Austrians at the top. One man identified the peaks for another one. At one point he hesitated—he did not know the name of a prominent summit before us. He turned to me: "Do you have any idea which one this is?" the Austrian asked. "It's the Olperer," I said, feeling like a million American dollars.

Stand there, beside the summit cross of Hafelekar, and see the Alps—the glaciers, the pastures, and man's settlements. Move your head slowly from east to west and cast your eyes to the medium-high middle foreground: this is the kingdom of the alps, above which the white peaks sit like crowns. On the pastures nearest your vision you will see cattle and chalets and villages, the houses huddling around a church steeple like chicks about a mother hen. Lower your gaze still further, and there is the elegant sweep of the Inn River running west-east through the city of Innsbruck.

There you stand by the big cross high above the city of Innsbruck, next to Toni. The stark barren Karwendel chain is at your back, but in front of you are a hundred miles of the main chain of "the Alps," a galaxy of summit after summit. Goethe's words, spoken by Faust are engraved there on a stone slab:

> Sublime Spirit, you gave me, gave me, everything I asked:
> You gave me Nature in her glory as my kingdom,
> Gave me the senses fully to embrace her, to enjoy.

It was here in Innsbruck, on one of my later trips, that the story of Joe Wurnitsch was anchored. It begins with a big crimson boot, cut out of steel like a guild sign of the Alpine countries, and fastened above the door of a cobbler's shop at Rose and Grove streets in Berkeley, California.

On a hunch, I walked into the shop. A woman customer was talking with a gaunt, white-haired man who critically looked at one of her shoes in his hand.

"Wouldn't last long, if I repaired it the way you want it," he said.

"But I want it that way," she said. "It's my shoe."

"Then do it yerself." He gave her the shoe and, without another look, sat down at his bench and resumed work on another shoe.

The woman left, shaking her head, and I started a conversation with Joe, one-way for a while. It turned out he was a Tirolean from a remote valley at the foot of the Grossglockner. He was seventy, and he had come to this country as a boy of sixteen. At first, he said, he had worked for a chain shoe-repair store. But not for long. "My boss always said to me not to fuss so much and to polish and push."

"What's 'polish and push'?"

"Means to shine up the shoe quick after the work was done, and to push it up on the shelf for the customer to pick up. Then do the next job in a hurry. No one cared whether the shoe would hold together another week."

Joe had learned the craft in his home village, in the mountains where you need shoes that will hold together. He did careful work, and that took too long for his employer. After three days of polish and push Joe had had enough.

When his boss hurried him again, he took off his green apron—Joe showed, as he talked, how he had lifted the strap over his head—and hung it on the hook.

"After that I got my own hole in the wall, and I've been here ever since."

I got to know him better in the months that followed. He was a free man—he did only work for those he liked. And he was a master craftsman. The most tricky jobs, especially ski and mountain boots, interested him most. He knew the human foot as well as any orthopedic doctor, and he merely needed to look at a shoe worn for a time to tell where it hurt and why—and how to fix it. In his independence and, indeed, in his appearance he was like the minnesinger Hans Sachs.

"Have you ever been back to your village in those fifty-four years" I asked him.

"No," said Joe leaning against his cash register, which would be the envy of the Smithsonian Institution.

"Any relatives there?"

"A brother in Hinterlingen. He doesn't write to me."

"Do you write to him?"

"No. We had a quarrel."

A quarrel (something about an inheritance) half a century old. I thought I detected a trace of regret in his voice but I couldn't tell. I asked him if I should visit his brother next time I got to the Alps.

"Hinterlingen is out of the way; in the Lenzinger valley, a dead end."

My first stop was Innsbruck. It's an incredible town. The Nordkette range rises directly behind the city, and the cableway goes to the Hafelekar on top. Where else in the world can you ski down a 7,000-foot mountain during your lunch hour, in winter? Thousands of Innsbruckers do. I walked down Maria Theresienstrasse, past restaurants and shops I had frequently patronized, past throngs of people in native dress—loden coats, dirndls, Tirolean skull caps. As always my first stop was at the Tyrolia Bookstore, but not to buy books. This store carries school texts and also "educational materials"—things like shells and minerals. I always buy their beautiful quartz crystals —those finest creations of nature. But that year they had nothing.

"You are too late, this year," said the salesman. "Our mountain people bring them in early spring, and when they're sold they're sold."

"You buy them from the peasants?"

"Yes. There aren't many left who know where to find them."

Naïvely I asked if he could put me in touch with one of those suppliers, so that I could get some specimens, or at least tell me in what part of the country those gems were found.

"We won't tell *that*, Mister. Come again next year."

I stopped at a store that sold those Edelweiss-and-gentian-decorated Tirolean skull caps you see in Innsbruck streets; they're handsome and "different," and easy to pack and take home as gifts. A little girl watched me buy some. "Do you like these?" I asked her. She shrugged. "They're all right, I guess, for the tourists." Didn't she wear them? "I? I'm a Tirolean."

I sat down in one of those delightful outdoor garden restaurants, so unaccountably rare in California, and ordered a meat dish. "With spinach?" said the waiter. "Why, yes, with spinach—how did you know?" "That's what you ordered last year." I had not even remembered that I had been to that restaurant before.

I could see what Joe had meant when he said his native valley was out of the way. Even the "main valley" I drove down to reach "his" valley was far removed from the track of the summer travelers. When I reached the Lenzinger valley, I had a feeling of being in some forgotten pocket of the Alpine world. The mountain road, just wide enough for a minicar, followed a lustily tumbling brook, cut in narrowly between mountain walls. There were few villages and scarcely any people on the road. The sense of remoteness was deepened by the semidarkness that hung between the high, deep-green, almost bluish walls of the narrow mountain valley. I had never been here before, yet I had a consciousness of "homecoming" to Joe's beautiful native valley, after more than a half century. I took pictures that I would show him when I returned. It was exciting to see a road sign indicating distances and including the name of Hinterlingen. The valley narrowed further and rose. Finally I reached a road sign: HINTERLINGEN.

I stopped and prepared to take a picture of it. Three old bearded men happened by and obligingly posed beside the sign, providing "human interest." I asked them if they knew a man by the name of Wurnitsch in that village.

"Yes. Up the road, the wooden farmhouse on the right."

I walked on. There was a stone wall on the right; I walked through an opening in it; behind it were a farmyard and a Tirolean-style gabled house. I knocked at a rough wooden door and a man opened it a crack. He looked like a prosperous farmer, wore coarse but good peasant clothing, and was the unmistakable younger edition of Joe Wurnitsch, cobbler in Berkeley. "What do you want?" he said without greeting.

"I am a friend of your brother," I said. "And I bring you greetings from him."

He stayed behind the crack. "Brother? I have no brother."

"You have a brother Joseph in America. I live in the same town, and he asked me to look you up."

"You are from America? Anybody could say that." The crack narrowed.

"But I am! I'll show you some papers, if you don't believe me, and I'll tell you things about your brother that no one else would know."

He asked me what I really wanted and I said I wanted the two brothers, half a world and half a century apart, to write to each other again. And to take a picture of him to show to Joe.

It was the wrong thing to say. "A picture, eh? I know that trick. There was a fellow here five years ago, taking pictures of everybody. Later he came back with the pictures and wanted money for them!"

"No, damn! I don't want money for the pictures. They're for free."

The crack widened. "They better be. And it won't do you any good if they aren't. I won't buy any."

I did not gain the man's complete confidence, but he softened up enough to come outside and allow me to sit beside him on the wooden bench before the door. He never asked me in, but I had a chance to explain and to take a picture. He remained cautious as I tried to make my point. Wasn't it a shame to have a brother in America and remain completely cut off? Did he know that his brother had been married for fifty years, had a daughter? Would he write to his brother now and let bygones be bygones?

No, he wouldn't.

Would he answer if his brother were to write to him?

He stared into the air. I said good-bye, and he did not shake hands, as would have been customary. But he saw me down the steps. Did he have a message for Joe?

"Tell him I'm all right."

"That's almost a letter," I said. "I'll tell him. And I'll send you a picture, then you'll believe me."

"I believe you. But don't charge me for it."

I walked around the village for a while. There was a small store with picture postcards, which I bought for Joe. And there was a shelf in that store with some beautiful quartz crystals—not for sale.

"You can buy some from Höfinger up the street," said the storekeeper. "He knows the places."

Höfinger's peasant house was a rock collector's dream. There shelf after shelf was filled with the jewels of the Alps, neatly kept on home-made trays. He was happy to sell them, pleased to have found somebody willing to buy. The next hour was like a treasure hunt in fairyland. Here were fine specimens usually seen only in museum cases— glass-clear clusters, delicately green-shaded columns, fine, perfectly pointed needles. We carefully wrapped each one in pieces of the local parish church newsletter, and I walked away, blissfully, laden with my heavy package. Not only did I feel like a treasure hunter who had struck it rich, but like a Maecenas who had poured dollar riches onto a poor peasant. "Did you ever sell that much to anybody?" I asked Höfinger on the doorstep. "Aw, yes. More than that. I sell my take every spring to the Tyrolia Bookstore in Innsbruck."

A month later, the cobbler in Berkeley passed the back of his peasant hand over his eyes to hide his emotions as he looked at my pictures from the Alps. So this was his valley. And this was the sign with the name of the village that wasn't on the map. And this, indeed, was his brother! Did he, by any chance, happen to know any of these three bearded men?

"This one," he said, "is my brother in law. And this

one is my other brother in law. And this one is my cousin.''

Was he kidding? How could he tell? He had not seen them in fifty-four years. They must have been youngsters then.

"I can tell," he just said. "I recognize 'em." He took the photographs, the picture postcards, and a map of the valley that I had brought, and some pressed leaves from a tree in his brother's yard, and stowed them all away under the counter. He gave me a look that was reward enough for a much greater effort than making a detour into the out-of-the-way Alpine valley.

The next day he wrote a postcard to his brother.

Inevitably, some day the tourists will discover the Lenzinger valley and Joe's home village; and perhaps some commercial enterprise, on a larger scale than old Höfinger's one-man business, will discover the supply source of the Tyrolia Bookstore in Innsbruck and try to exploit the crystal locations in Hinterlingen. But I won't help them—the story is true, but the names are fictitious.

Joe, though, is not fictitious. If you need a job that calls for a master of the art of leather craft, see him at Rose and Grove, where the crimson boot hangs out. If you can win his favor he will do anything for you. And ask him whether he has heard recently from his brother in the Alps.

A huntsman falls and Theuerdank crosses the slope by another route

6. The First Time

IN THE MOUNTAINS between the Stubai and Oetz valleys—between the same two huts where I had met the two German students and the guide Salchner on my original return trip—our son Martin had his day on one of the later trips. He was eleven then. Both he and his brother Anthony had been on mountain trips in the Sierra Nevada since they were very young. There had been one Sierra trip when Martin's short legs (he was seven at the time, Anthony eleven) did not seem to be able to make the top. Anthony ambled boldly ahead but Martin was desperate and close to giving up when the leader of the party, Cliff Youngquist, mountaineer and small-boy psychologist, discovered what was happening. Along with lunch and sweater and first-aid kit he had some red feathers in his pack. Martin had noticed that several boys in the party proudly wore such feathers on their hats. They were prizes that Cliff had awarded to those who had earned them on earlier trips. Now, seeing Martin's distress, he announced that a red feather would be awarded to all those under ten who reached the top. Martin did not realize that he was the only candidate, the youngest in the party, but the red feather did the trick, together with some active support by Cliff who stayed with Martin and navigated him over some big boulders. He did reach the top and he earned the feather, and for years it was the symbol of his achievement. He still had it on his hat when we set out on a family trip in the Alps, aiming at glacier-bound Zuckerhütl ("Sugar Loaf"), 11,520 feet, highest peak in the Stubai Alps.

He had done well on several lower peaks, so we thought we would try him out at least part of the way, even though we probably would not attempt to take him to the top. Our plan was first to follow the same route to the two huts that I had taken years earlier, leave him at the second hut, and have him wait there for our return from the Zuckerhütl. We hoped, however, that Anthony would be able to make the top—the guide would decide.

No rain was falling this time as we strolled up to the first hut, where we had our scrambled pancakes ten years earlier. But the meadows were as rich and abundant as then, and the euphoria I had felt then was now shared by my wife Charlotte and the boys. Martin expressed it his own way. He threw his arms up into the air ("like peppermint," as Anthony had said), flapped them up and down and shouted "I'm free as a bird!" We stopped at a "Sennhütte" along the way for large glasses of milk.

My dictionary renders Sennhütte soberly as "Alpine dairy." It is the primitive chalet where the herdsman (Senner) or herdswoman (Sennerin) lives, who takes care of the cattle during the summer.

After four hours we reached the first hut. There we spent the night—or as much of it as our guide allowed. He roused us at 3:30 A.M. You have to get up early when you are on Alpine tours—either because you want to see the sunrise or because you want to walk over the snow before the sun softens it and makes walking difficult. Mark Twain, awakened early by a guide, in an Alpine hut, when it was "dark and cold and wretched," commented gloomily: "I thought of how many happy people there were in Europe, Asia, and America, and everywhere, who were sleeping peacefully in their beds and did not have to get up and see the sunrise."

Although twenty-seven other guides were available, by one of those coincidences that are taboo in novels but happen in real life, the guide who woke us was the same man, Johann Salchner, who had led me from hut one to hut two ten years earlier. Slowly we crossed from the green zone to the white zone toward the snow-free spot on top that divides the Stubai valley from the Oetz valley. But this time it was Anthony who puffed and Martin who marched ahead. Salchner watched the four of us, and I sensed that he was sizing us up for the next day when we should begin our assault on the Zuckerhütl after spending the night in the second hut.

The second hut had not changed in the years between—a refreshingly simple, welcoming island shelter in the icy world around us. We dried our snow-soaked shoes and socks by the warm stove and went to bed early. The next morning we would not be descending through Shangri-la to the Oetz valley, but climbing up the Zuckerhütl.

Martin had kept up with the guide all day as we crossed the glacier between the two huts. In the evening I asked the guide what he thought of Anthony's coming along to the top on the morrow. "He has short breath," pronounced Salchner; "he had better wait in the hut until we get back." Then, pointing to Martin: "But this one's OK."

It turned out that Anthony was more relieved than disappointed but Martin was popping with pride. He passed his hand over the red feather on his hat. "Good old Cliff," he said.

Up at 5 A.M. and start at 6. The host lent us ski poles to help us through the snow. Then we trooped up the

Pfaffenferner ("Parson's glacier") as Anthony, watching us from the hut, became smaller until he and the hut disappeared when we turned a corner.

For two hours we tramped the glacier. It was covered with snow, and no cracks could be seen, but the guide sometimes avoided the straight line of ascent as if he wanted to skirt a spot he knew was dangerous. The sun came out and baked our faces, with double exposure of rays above and reflection from the snow below. The glow soon permeated skin and body, and there was a sense of jubilant freedom, heightened as we shed our outer wraps. Nothing stood between the vast expanse of the untouched glacier and the stainless sky except the four of us. The brilliance of the day conveyed a sensation of weightlessness and infinite space such as astronauts might feel. As we gained altitude we felt we were mastering destiny, and an exhilarating sense of power and youth filled us.

Martin did not stray from the side of the guide, although the snow became softer as the hours passed, and the effort of pulling a short leg from the snow is greater than that of pulling a long one. At 8:30 A.M. we reached the saddle from which towered, like a sugarloaf indeed, the three-sided pyramid of the Zuckerhütl.

From the saddle we were looking at two of the three faces of the pyramid. The left face was snow-free, rocky and black; the right face was covered by snow, soft at this hour, and silky white; the two faces came together at a vertical knife-edge ridge, sharp as if drawn by a ruler and still covered by snow. We looked up: our route would be directly at the ridge, in the snow.

Suddenly the sun vanished, and we were instantly cold. We cocooned ourselves into our padded windbreakers and Martin slipped into his red parka and hood, looking like an elf. We took the packs off our backs and left them at the saddle. The guide pulled a rope from his pack and lashed it around us with the matter-of-factness of a man who knows his stuff. He was first, followed by Martin, Charlotte, and me. Slowly we started out from the saddle, level for a few steps until it began to rise toward the summit pyramid. Within moments clouds and shreds of fog, as if attracted by a huge magnet, gathered around the peak before us, hiding it now, freeing it a minute later to permit a glimpse of the cross on top.

The rope was pulled tightly around us in our thick wraps. "I feel like a mummy," said Martin. Nevertheless, I felt free and safe, trusting the guide. Single file we trudged up, ever steeper. Now the guide began to use his ax to cut toeholds in the snow, which was hardening. We had to keep an even pace between us because the rope must never become slack. Every few minutes we paused,

and I looked back at our tracks. They did not disturb the otherwise untouched beauty of the snow, but seemed to define its nature. I remembered that I had seen these same snowtracks through Toni Schlechtleitner's telescope from the Hafelekar, and wondered whether he would be looking at us now. I also remembered photographs showing human tracks in snow broken by Arctic explorers—the vastness, the unfathomable silence seemed to have been brought to life by the tracks. We were directly at the knife's edge, and our footsteps cut a pearly pattern in it. To take steps was tough work now, and we concentrated on the toe holes in the hardened snow. Two-thirds of the way up, we rested on our feet.

The solid cover of icy snow was broken on top by some boulders, whipped clean by storms. This last pitch was the steepest, and we moved slowly when we started again. Now we had to stop after each step, making sure that we had a firm hold. To our left was the black rock face of the pyramid, to the right the flawless spread of the white face, the white also covering the knife edge on which we were walking. Every step clearly reduced the remaining distance from the top. The cross loomed directly overhead, separated from us only by the boulders which we had now reached. There was some commotion ahead of me, as the guide stepped aside and called something to Martin that I could not understand. Then I saw what was happening. Martin passed the guide who had taken a firm stand on the boulders; he wanted Martin to reach the cross first.

And so it was. Seconds later, Martin, with a muffled yell, grabbed the post of the towering cross—in my mind I saw him planting a red feather at the top. We scrambled after him over the rocks and sat down beside the heavy wires that held the cross firmly fastened to the summit of the Zuckerhütl.

Here we were, cold and wet and played out, and we felt the pressure of the rope that the guide did not take off because we would need it later. Yet this was the moment of consummation.

I rested the back of my head against the base of the solid cross and I felt the sun on my burnished skin. What was it now that gave me this profound upswelling of glory? Part of it, I thought, was that I shared at this moment in the ultimate encounter between man and earth; that there is in man a deep-seated yearning for the ultimate, for the end, for the absolute, for the eternal. In *The Book of the Mountains*, a symposium edited by A.C. Spectorsky, a contribution entitled "Why Men Climb" contains the sentences: "Whatever man's passion for conquering the highest peaks may mean symbolically, it has a plain and simple, literal meaning: the impulse, informing all our culture, which has driven the Western world toward the limits of human experience. To stand at the highest point is to occupy such a limit. Here ends the human world, farther one cannot go." Some men have this inner experience of the ultimate as they face the immensity of the ocean. I have been told that people who grew up in the puszta, the grassy, horizon-defying flatlands of Hungary, have an explosive experience when they again see the vast expanse of those plains after a long absence from their homeland.

Had I grown up by the ocean shore or in the plains, I would probably share such feelings. But I have not, and although the waters and prairies speak to me, they do not stir me. I am awed by the play of untamed waves on a rocky shore, but I am *moved* by the sight of quiet mountains and by the resplendent primeval beauty of their covers of verdant pastures or dazzling glaciers.

In his "Ode to Joy," which Beethoven apotheosized in his Ninth Symphony, Schiller calls out in ecstasy, "Be embraced, ye millions!" and flings a "kiss to the whole world." Around us, here, were the pinnacles of my youth, there was my wife in her first visit to the Alps, and my young son in whom the love for these mountains was beginning to bloom like a precious plant. These were the mountains of the land where I was born, but there was no "patriotism" in my feelings. I had left my homeland not of my own free will but had been driven out in the thirties by evil men, who had lived in these same mountains and were my "compatriots." Many of them, with blood on their hands, still lived there—our guide had told me how he had hidden from them in the mountains during the last weeks of the war. Whatever men do, the mountains are innocent, and what I felt as I rested on the crown of that mountain was not restricted to the mountains of Austria but embraced all the Alps—of Switzerland, Italy, or France. I cannot deny that I have a "native" feeling of being in tune with the very air in these mountains, a feeling that I do not have in the mountains of other continents, much as I like to explore them too; but this native feeling has no national overtones. Be embraced ye millions in all lands, co-sailors on this earth raft in space.

I realized that I had my eyes closed, and I opened them now. Yes, the view. The fickle weather charitably allowed us a view for short periods. The tracks we had cut on our way up seemed to link us, like an umbilical cord, with the rest of the world below. Across from us lay a gently rounded mountaintop, spotlessly white and glistening when the sun caught it between clouds. The closer peaks

stood out in dark relief, those behind were less distinct, and the still farther ones paled as they receded into the horizon. I was reminded of some Japanese paintings that show the color gradations of these mountainscapes. The sun was in such a position that some peaks cast their shadows against the delicate white of the snow, as if enormous dark aprons had been laid upon it. The contrast between light and shadow, white and black were dramatic and sharp. There are no doubts in these mountains, there are absolutes even in the colors.

It was completely still. I heard my own breathing. I looked over at Martin, who had his head slightly turned. When he saw my glance he whispered: "I'm listening to the silence."

The guide, Salchner, was last as we began to climb down; Martin was now first. We started down with our faces to the mountain, using our former toe holes. The snow had by now turned almost entirely to ice. The slope seemed precipitously steep as we descended, and I had a hollow feeling in my stomach every time I tried to get a foothold but seemed to be probing glass. The old toe holes were not always where I needed them, or they were too small, and I missed the guide cutting new holes with his ice ax. I felt he should be ahead of us. After a short and uneasy while he said that we should turn around, with our backs to the mountain. I tried to do this, which meant that I had to let go of one toe hold and swivel around on the other; also I had to remove my hands from the slope. I detached myself from my precarious face-to-mountain position, and slipped. All holds gone, I began to roll down the slope, lying crosswise against it. But with the swiftness of a cheetah the guide pulled the rope tight, standing firmly above me. He then stepped closer, pulling in the rope as he approached so that it remained tight, and helped me up. He said nothing. I no longer wished that he were ahead rather than behind.

It was a relief to reach the packs and take off the rope. The short descent to the saddle had been the most tense minutes of our expedition. The most lighthearted moments followed as we happily walked down the way we had laboriously climbed. The satisfaction of accomplishment seemed to give wings to our ankles and speed us on. Martin, especially, hopped along like a young goat. After two hours, the silence, broken only by our own footsteps, was suddenly rent by a loud yodel—and there was Anthony, who had walked a little way up from the hut to meet us. With a mock bow he presented Martin with a black feather from a mountain crow.

7. Crystals and Graves

WHEN YOU ARRIVE at the Oetz valley after a Zuckerhütl expedition, you can follow the new Alpine automobile road across the Timmelsjoch pass into the world of the Dolomites in Italy; or you can reach them by returning to Innsbruck and either driving or riding the train over the Brenner pass. The Dolomites include some of the most spectacular peaks of the Alps, and their cession to Italy after the First World War was one of the most painful losses for Austria. The wounds still have not healed. Italy, after a stubborn resistance, has granted a good measure of autonomy to the 230,000 German-speaking people in the region—road signs are in both languages and many maps show the names of peaks translated: Villabassa/Niederdorf, Monteguelfo/Wolfsberg, Palla Bianca/Weisskugel, Pausabella/Schönrast, Gran Pilastro/Hochfeiler. But Austrian nationalist terrorists have been active in the area and have injected a note of irresponsibility in the continuing negotiations between Italy and Austria that are designed to consider grievances. In 1969 an agreement was reached by the two governments in Copenhagen; Italy promised to increase self-government and to allow greater use of German as an official language, in steps to be taken within four years; and to change the Italian name of the province, Alto Adige, back to the original German Südtirol.

Crossing the Austrian-Italian border at the Brenner means crossing from a relatively unspoiled area, although defiled along the road by hand-printed anti-Italian hate slogans, into an area defaced by commercial billboards. Such advertisements are banned on the Austrian side, but the Italians have plastered all access to the Dolomites with them. On one occasion I tried to take photographs of Lake Misurina, one of the treasures of the Dolomites, and was unable to get the mountain backgrounds I wanted without some plug for sewing-machines or gasoline.

South of the Brenner pass, the Isarco valley leads to Bolzano. Halfway down, the Gardena (Gröden) valley branches off on the east side. This valley, with its principal town, Ortisei (St. Ulrich), is the center for woodcarvers whose wares can be seen all over Italy and Austria and are also exported to the United States. As I entered the township, I saw man-size angels stacked like cordwood on a one-wheel pushcart standing unattended at a main street curb, their arms grotesquely raised to the sky— *horizontally.* Souvenir shops displaying wood-carved saints, madonnas, bottle stoppers, peasant figurines, and multiantlered deer were all over town.

The shop owners were bilingual, responding in Italian when you said "Buon giorno" or in German when you said "Grüss Gott." Among themselves they spoke Ladin, also used in a linguistic enclave in the Engadine valley of Switzerland; it is one of two dialects of Romansch, a derivative of Latin—the other dialect being Rhaeto-Romansch spoken in the Swiss Rhine valley. Many signs, such as those in the townhall, were in all three languages. An official in the townhall told me that Ladin was the first language children spoke at home; at school they learned German and Italian simultaneously. This seemed a difficult feat to me, but, clearly, the natives had no trouble. In addition, there are evidently enough tourists so that some townspeople speak a little English as well. I was told that inscriptions, store signs, and the like were permitted in German, but the Italian version alongside of it was mandatory. You could paint the word "Gasthof" above the door of your inn, so long as it was preceded by the word "Albergo"; the addition of the word in Ladin was optional. Personal first names were required to be Italianized, hence Johann had to be Giovanni. I photographed a grocery store that piquantly sported the owner's name as "Cristiano Schmalzl"—a delicacy German-speaking readers will appreciate.

Ortisei, at the base of the impressive Sasso Lungo (Langkofel) massif, is also a celebrated skiing area in winter. But I had not come to ski, buy carved bottle stoppers, or study languages. I wanted to hunt for geodes —hollow rock spheres, inconspicuous on the outside but lined with delicious quartz or amethyst crystals when they are split open.

After asking around in town for a while, I was directed to see Enrico (Heinrich) Moroder, a wood carver, painter of carvings, member of an old family of local wood carvers, and an amateur rockhound. I found him in his shop, his sons carving, and himself painting a crèche. I confirmed that Moroder, 60, with an artist's mane of white hair, was a passionate rock collector. For years he had scoured the Dolomites, and the window sills and shelves in his shop were filled with the trophies of his expeditions. He was immediately game for a trip the next day, and told me that he had led geologists of the University of Ferrara and had donated many excellent finds—including shell, plant, and fish fossils—to museums and college collections. He refused an offer of payment; he was only too pleased to exchange his paint brush and carving knife for a geological hammer and accompany a fellow rock nut.

High above the floor of the Gardena valley is a great shelf, a grassy plateau, the Alpe di Siusi (Seiser Alpe). It is a world of its own, reached either by a cableway from Ortisei or, from the back end, by a road from the town of Siusi (Seis). We took the first trip on the cableway in the early morning of this clean-scrubbed day in late June and found ourselves in a wildflower meadow that, surely, was patterned after the Garden of Eden. For three hours we walked across those millions of gentians, Alpenrosen, larkspur, wild yellow pansies, brunellas, and, especially near the many brooks, forget-me-nots and filled buttercups (trollflowers). In some places they were all mixed together, so that we could have picked a large colorful bouquet of different flowers from the same spot; in others they formed one-flower tapestries. We saw a field covered exclusively by white crocus and another by abundant, metallic-blue, single-bell gentians—they all seemed to grow equidistant from each other like a pattern on a peasant skirt. "A little girl once told me," said Moroder, "that when the Lord made the Seiser Alpe, he accidentally spilled the flower-filled basket he had prepared for supplying the flowers for all the meadows of the Alps." The Alps are rich with flowery meadows, but my prize for the lushest of all goes to the Seiser Alpe.

Moroder offered to take me on a side tour for Edelweiss, those rarest and most precious of the Alpine flora; but this side trip would have made it impossible for us to reach our goal and return the same day. Our goal was a series of dramatically rugged, bare, reddish mountain spires squatting on the far end of the plateau. Moroder called them Rosszähne (horses' teeth), a corruption of the Italian Denti di Terrarossa (red-earth teeth). "We do not have to climb the Rosszähne themselves," Moroder explained, "but the steep hill before them—we'll have plenty of work."

As I looked at those grotesque "teeth" formations, it became clear why one of the Alpine pioneers, Leslie Stephen, an Englishman, and at one time president of the British Alpine Club, writing in *The Playground of Europe*, called the Dolomites "the fairyland of the Alps." In a passage referring to some "singular peaks" in the Dolomites, he says: "I compared the ridge before me to some monstrous reef, stretching out to seaward with a singularly daring lighthouse erected on a distant point . . . or to the head of some great monster extended to full length, and armed with a couple of curved horns like those of a double-horned rhinoceros." Fairyland indeed.

We followed the currents of several small wild brooks to climb the trackless hills, sometimes using boulders in the brooks to gain altitude. The brooks came from the crest of the chain of hills. We were now 8,000 feet high, and there was little vegetation. These hills were our collecting area, and I kept my eyes on the ground. Slowly we worked our way up the cuts through which the brooks came down, from time to time probing the sides for geodes. Then, of a sudden, I saw one stuck loosely in the side of the cut—I could simply lift it without using my geology pick. Triumphantly I handed it to Moroder, who was hanging, somewhat precariously, above me in the cut —using one hand to balance himself on a boulder, the other to dig in the soil. "I got one," I called out. "You passed it up!" Moroder took a look at the rock ball in his hand, then, to my dismay, threw it down the mountainside.

I gasped for a second, and felt like giving him a push to roll down after it. "Why the hell did you do *that*?"

"There weren't any crystals inside," said Moroder.

"You didn't even look!" I protested. "How could you know, you did not split it open!"

Whereupon he made the classic pronouncement: "When they're full, they're empty."

By weighing the ball in his hand he could tell that it was too heavy to be hollow. Many geodes are just filled solid with ordinary rock. They have no crystals.

I still had doubts. We climbed on, and shortly after I found another. "Don't throw this one away. Tell me if it's full or hollow."

He felt it for a second only. "Full."

I rearranged my stance to have my hands free, then broke my find with my hammer. True and frustrating enough: it was just a stone ball, "full," hence empty of crystals. Moroder knew his rocks.

But the disappointment did not last long. Soon, as we approached the crest, I found a large, curved fragment studded excitingly with amethyst tips, clear and sparkling, a rich reward for the labors of the day. He also found some, and soon we picked them up left and right, just lightly scratching the sidewalls of the cut in which the brook flowed downhill, We wrapped the fragile fragments like eggshells in the tissue we had brought along for this purpose, and gradually filled our packs. They got heavier and heavier.

For three hours we stayed in those hills. Then we decided to return in order to reach the cableway before dark. Happily we scrambled down the hillsides, then waded again through the flower meadows. When we reached Ortisei, Moroder tapped my bulging heavy rucksack. "When it's full," he said this time, "it's full."

One of the finest views in the Dolomites is said to be from Monte Piano near famed Lake Misurina—toward the Tre Cime (Drei Zinnen) and a large part of the Dolomite ranges. I set out from Misurina to see the view—I never did, but the experience was, perhaps, more memorable than the missed view.

Where the road to that mountain began, a marker said: TO THE BATTLEFIELDS. Following a road identified by blue paint patches on rocks for about an hour, I reached the Bosi hut at 7,000 feet. I had known that it was an easy walk, and I had not bothered to change into my mountain boots. I ought to have known better—you don't walk in the Alps in oxfords, not even on "easy" hikes.

I bought a drink at the hut, but did not stay and continued further uphill. Soon it became clear that this was historical ground. Almost a half century after the First World War I found the evidence of man's ferocity all over the area—rusty helmets, parts of rifles, field kitchens, spades for trench digging, chunks of boots. A small canteen, pierced by bayonets, was silent testimony to the fierce man-to-man slaughter that had taken place here between Austrian and Italian mountain troops.

I was standing at a rolling plateau with hills superimposed on the shelf. Deep trenches ran in all directions, seemingly at random; many were lined at the top by rusty pieces of barbed wire. In several places were tombstones and monuments on that hilly plateau; grenade shells served as flower vases, helmets as decorations. My attention was absorbed by these sights and I forgot about the view—I could not have seen it anyway, because of the clouds and ragged wisps of fog. Then it started to rain, and since I had only a light jacket I decided to turn back.

I started in the direction from which I had come. The area was rocky and without plant life—a desolation fitting for this place of death. Somehow I lost track of the blue markers that led back to the hut and to Misurina. I changed my direction to find them again but was not sure where the last marker was that I had seen. The fog had become thicker, the scene looked the same in every direction—rocks, hilly mounds, trenches. It was getting rapidly colder; the rain turned into snowy sleet, turning the ground into a wet morass. I looked around . . .

And I realized I was lost.

I deliberated for a while, then chose the direction in which I vaguely assumed the last markers may have been. Besides, I knew I had to go downhill. But the terrain was not level, and what was downhill for a while turned uphill later. At one point I found myself at the edge of the plateau, at a cliff unexpectedly going straight down into nowhere, and I had to go back.

Walking became difficult. The slush seeped into my shoes. Still no markers. The blue markings had been dabbed on various slabs, some flat on the ground, some sticking out higher. Soon the lower rocks were covered by snow, and my markers with them. I pinned my hopes on the few larger rocks, but with the cold and the snow I was aware of something else creeping into me: fear.

Nobody knew where I was, no one would miss me. I had arrived in Misurina at noon, left my pack in an inn "for a couple of hours," planning to be back in the late afternoon; the maid in that inn would hardly get excited about a rucksack that some stranger had left and not picked up when he said he would. It began to get dark. I changed my direction several times, fooled by trenches that sometimes looked like trails. I had visions of spending the night up here and looked into those trenches for possible shelter. But they were half filled by a muddy broth of snow water, and I thought of the soldiers who stood in them, up to the hips in water . . .

I was thoroughly wet myself as I stamped along in the snow. In the semi-darkness I hardly expected to recognize markers even on large rocks anymore. Wasn't there a living soul in these mountains? After all, the hut could not be far away—perhaps a half mile, I calculated.

It was then that I saw footprints in the snow, and I perked up. I held my gaze fixed on them, so as not to lose them, also making sure that I did not mix them with my own, so that I could check back if necessary. The tracks led to trenches, followed them briefly, then backed away. I walked faster, the water squishing in my shoes. The direction of the tracks changed a few times . . . and finally I recognized them as my own tracks.

I stopped and made inventory. I was not going to panic, I said to myself. In about a half hour it would be night. I was wet, cold, hungry, unequipped, and had not registered or left word where I was going. I had behaved like one of those Sunday excursionists whom I had warned so many times before. I was an idiot.

I scanned the horizon for any possible trace of human beings. For a moment I thought I was hallucinating when I actually saw, outlined on a hill against the dusky sky, shadowy figures, moving slowly. I shouted, but the sound was muffled in the rain and snow, and I doubted that my voice had carried up there. But the figures, although apparently not standing still, did not move away, and so I started to run and stumble toward them, up the hill. I kept shouting—why did they not answer? I saw them so indistinctly that I wondered whether these might be animals after all—chamois? Crazy idea. No, these were humans, three of them, wearing long cloaks against the rain; I could make out the peaked hoods on their heads. Perhaps they were lost too, but I was no longer alone, I was saved.

When I reached the hill, there were three graves. Pointed stone monuments silently holding watch over the soldiers buried there.

I felt my heart miss a beat. There were the "peaked hoods" I had seen. The "slow movements" must have been an illusion produced by the moving fog and my own motions as I had advanced.

I leaned against the monuments and took great pains in deciphering the names in the dark as if they could hold clues to getting back. Then I decided to be "rational." I might have to spend a long night right here. There was no shelter anywhere, not even a tree or overhanging rock. It was snowing furiously now. I knew I would not fall asleep during the night. There was no danger of that now —although I was painfully tired, I was feverishly awake.

I searched my pockets. No, I did not have a match. Nor was there anything with which to build a fire. But I found my mountain whistle, always with me in the Alps.

The Alpine emergency call: six signals (acoustic or visual) per minute, one every ten seconds; then one minute silence; then six signals again, and so on. I had known it since childhood, never seriously expected to be in a position to use it myself. Why had I not thought of it till now? I had a watch. When I held it very close to my eyes I could read it in the dark.

It was a relief to hear my own whistle cutting through the night. I waited ten seconds, then blew it again. Six times per minute. The minute of silence was long, but I could see now what a wise thing it was to have established the signal just that way. It relieves the man in distress from gluing his eye to his watch without any rest. It breaks the terrible monotony of waiting. It gives him time to listen.

It turned out that I did not have to wait long. A dim light appeared in the dark—this time it was really a human figure that emerged. The hut had been just around the corner. The caretaker had remembered that I had checked in on the way up, and he had casually wondered whether I would check in on the way back. When he heard the whistle, he guessed who it was.

"Excursionists," he muttered.

Theuerdank saved by his climbing-irons on a mossy slope.

8. Wandern in the Oberland

FROM THE DOLOMITES, several routes lead to Switzerland, the central portion of the Alps. Never did I feel more in tune with the world than when as a teenager I "wandered" and hitchhiked from Italy to Switzerland; and again when I was a man wandering in the Bernese Oberland.

The German word *wandern* is rendered inadequately in English as "to wander" or "to hike." "To wander" has overtones of aimlessness, and "to hike" of purposefulness. *Wandern* is done with an aim—you usually know where you are going; but it is unregimented and, although not necessarily leisurely, dominated by your mind, not your legs. Thoreau liked to think of himself not as a walker or hiker but as a "saunterer," and "to saunter" is perhaps one aspect of *wandern*. German romantic poetry has Wanderlust as one of its principal themes, and there is good reason for using the word, untranslated, in American English. *Wandern*, furthermore, has medieval echoes. In the life style of the guilds, the craftsman, after he had finished his apprenticeship, would "go out into the world" as *Wanderbursche*, his pack on his back, before he would settle down after his *Wanderschaft* and become, literally, a journey man. "Das Wandern ist des Müllers Lust," wrote nineteenth-century German romantic poet Joseph von Eichendorff, who had "wandered" along Alpine valleys from Germany to Austria and whose verses Schubert set to music for the wanderers of later generations. *Wandern* means yearning for the big, wide world, the next corner, the next view, the great unknown, brotherhood, adventure, beauty, life. The classic era of *Wanderschaft* was the time before the advent of the automobile, but it is not yet over in the Alps, and *Wandervögel* (birds of passage, ramblers), young and old, find those Alpine roads where automobiles either cannot go or are infrequent enough to be ignored. In fact, modern young people have made a compromise; they hitchhike to the places where they start their undisturbed trail-wandering. In my student days, when I "supplemented" my *wandern* in the Alps with hitchhiking, the practice was still a novelty in Europe and considered a thrilling American import; automobiles were for the rich, and too few to threaten mountain roads.

At that time I hitchhiked twice over the Italian-Swiss border: once over the Stelvio pass, then, at 9,055 feet, Europe's highest automobile road, and a second time over the Bernina pass.

There had been an automobile race the day I hitchhiked over the Stelvio. The driver of a racing car, on his way home, gave me a lift from the pass. The car was roofless, and my seat, perhaps to reduce weight, had had its upholstery removed. I sat on two steel bars as the driver tore down the forty-eight hairpin curves through the icy fog. The drive allowed only occasional glimpses of the mighty Ortler at one side, once Austria's highest peak (12,802 feet). It had been explored by the Austrian Arctic pioneer, Julius von Payer, in the nineteenth century. But I had little thought for the historical aspects of my trip nor could I appreciate the technical achievement represented by the road, considered a great feat when it was built in 1824. I held on for dear life, while the two steel bars cut into my native upholstery as I was rammed down against them at each curve. The happy ordeal ended when we reached the Engadine valley, and although I was sore all over, it had been a colorful crossing of the Alps.

The second time, when I hitchhiked across the Bernina pass to St. Moritz, was less dramatic but more romantic. The summits along the pass road had exciting names—Piz Bernina, Piz Palü, Diavolezza—but I had mixed feelings when the driver, who had picked me up at the Italian-Swiss border station, dropped me at the edge of St. Moritz, retreat of kings and celebrities. Here I was, the bum, facing with awed disgust the hotel palaces, those impregnable fortresses of luxury. Of course I had no intention or means of entering them, but it was late in the day and I wondered where I would spend the night. Just then two sun-tanned girls, packs on their backs, walked by, with the familiar tired-hopeful stride of mountaineers returning from a trip. I called to them and they stopped.

"Are you coming from a tour?"

"Yes. The Diavolezza."

"Where are you headed now?"

"For the Jugendherberge."

The youth-hostel system was well developed even then. Today it is a sprawling network of inexpensive places for young people to stay overnight when they tour the mountains. The hostels are strategically spaced to allow young travelers more flexibility in choosing their itineraries. Some hostels are, or were then, situated simply in a peasant's hayloft, others were in schoolhouses, churches, or other large buildings. I saw recently, in Zell am See, an impressive building with a heartwarming atmosphere, directly by the lake, the dormitories equipped with showers, and meals provided by a resident staff.

The hostel in St. Moritz was plain but its location by the lakeshore superb. The place swarmed with young people telling about their experiences in half a dozen languages, striking up friendships, sharing food warmed on coin-operated gas burners. Most young men and women were wanderers—they had come on foot; some were hitchhikers, others had traveled on bicycles. There was relaxed, accepting comradship; the tanned faces still radiated warmth in the hostel commons after sundown.

A young Frenchman sat down on the doorstep of the hostel facing the lake and played his guitar. Presently we were all gathered around him singing the songs of many lands that were the cultural heritage of our generation— we all knew them and joined in. We had never met before and would disperse in all directions tomorrow, yet on that evening we were a family. We shared our youth, freedom to come and go, thrill of the adventurous tomorrow, the afterglow of the day's experience in the mountains, the skin-close proximity of the opposite sex as we sat around the guitar player.

After the Second World War, I resumed my *wandern* in Switzerland. If walking in my youth had been "softened" by hitchhiking, it now was softened by occasional rides on cableways which, as a student, I had scorned or could not afford. Cableways to mountain summits were invented by devils but will take you where the angels sing.

Many summers I walked the trails of the Rhone valley, the Rhine valley, and the Inn or En valley (the Engadine), but most frequently I walked in the Bernese Oberland, the region between the trench formed by the twin lakes of Brienz and Thun, and the storied ice-sheathed ranges north of the Rhone.

"Neither Chamouni nor Zermatt is equal in grandeur and originality of design to the Bernese Oberland," wrote Leslie Stephen. He continued:

"No earthly object that I have seen approaches in grandeur to the stupendous mountain wall whose battlements overhang in mid-air the villages of Lauterbrunnen and Grindelwald; the lower hills that rise beneath it, like the long Atlantic rollers beaten back from the granite cliffs on our western coast, are a most effective contrast to its stern magnificence; in the whole Alps there is no ice-stream to be compared to the noble Aletsch glacier, sweeping in one majestic curve from the crest of the ridge down to the forests of the Rhone valley; no mountains, not even the aiguilles of Mont Blanc, or the Matterhorn itself, can show a more graceful outline than the Eiger— that monster, as we may fancy, in the act of bounding

from the earth; and the Wetterhorn, with its huge basement of cliffs contrasted with the snowy cone that soars so lightly into the air above, seems to me to be a very masterpiece in a singularly difficult style; but indeed every one of the seven familiar summits, whose very names stand alone in the Alps for poetical significance—the Maiden, the Monk, the Ogre, the Storm Pike, the Terror Pike, and the Dark Aar Pike—would each repay the most careful study of the youthful designer. Four of these, the Jungfrau, Mönch, Eiger, and Wetterhorn, stand like watchhouses on the edge of the cliffs."

The classic way of enjoying a mountain is to climb it, as I have done so many times in the Austrian Alps. The romantic way is to walk around a mountain as one would around a fine statue, to savor it from all sides. I like this kind of *wandern* in the Oberland; it is especially suited for the Swiss mountains. Unlike the Austrian Alps, which are essentially a series of east-west chains, the Swiss Alps are a jigsaw puzzle of massifs connected by a sophisticated network of passes; the wanderer, by crossing one after another of these passes in circles, is allowed to gain a view of the other side of the peaks.

As I walked the Swiss trails I reached points from which I could look back at places where I had been—triangulation points that finally formed a map in my mind. When the jigsaw-puzzle pieces of familiar landscapes fell into place, I felt a delicious familiarity with the composite picture of valleys and summits. Among my triangulation points in the Oberland are the village of Reuti, the Big Scheidegg pass, the lookout from the summit terminal of the Schilthorn cableway, the Schynige Platte, and Lake Oeschinen.

The Wetterhorn, seen between the triangulation points of Reuti and Big Scheidegg pass, holds a special magic for me. It is certainly the peer of its neighbors, the Eiger-Mönch-Jungfrau triad. From the Brünig pass, a rail link between Lucerne and Interlaken, a six-mile road leads past Goldern and dead-ends at Reuti. Even though the mail bus rattles noisily through Reuti every day, it still remains a charming, unspoiled village. The road is cut into a mountain shelf parallel to the main highway far below in the Hasli valley. The highway goes through the town of Meiringen and over a couple of passes to Italy. Down there travels the world's traffic. Up here, on the Reuti shelf, undisturbed nature has a living chance so long as the road remains a dead end.

Each time I walk from the Brünig pass to Reuti, I think of the guild journeymen. At the beginning the road leads through dim forest, then the view opens onto meadows stretching down into the Hasli valley. I always stop at Goldern, at the German refugee high school, École d' Humanité, founded by the saintly Paul Geheeb after he fled from Nazi oppression. Although it counts well-known names among its alumni (Thomas Mann's son, Nehru's grandchildren), it is not a school for the privileged, but is open to children of all lands and of all stations, and its message is the worth of man everywhere —a "school of humanity." Instruction is in German and English, with a good measure of French; the youngsters pick up languages easily and soon switch casually from one to the other. I do not know of a school in a more spectacular setting. It is dominated by the jagged, glacier-blanketed Wetterhorn and surrounded by the flower-studded alps of the Alps. The children who grow up here will be the richer, no doubt, for having lived part of their lives in this beautiful land. Even if they come from distant countries, they feel they belong here, and think of it as their second home long after they have returned to their native lands—as I learned from Anthony and Martin, who also attended, and now fondly remember, Paul Geheeb's school.

The Wetterhorn's three arresting peaks (the highest, 12,166 feet) have lured mountain lovers since the beginning of systematic exploration of the Alps in the middle of the nineteenth century. Englishmen—Eardley J. Blackwell and Justice Alfred Wills—were the first to reach the summit, both in 1854.

My most memorable trip around the Wetterhorn began with a rather shorter-than-expected conversation with a peasant at Reuti. I had arrived there after leaving Goldern behind, and stopped at a Swiss peasant chalet, which was covered by wisteria vines. The owner sat on a wooden bench in front, whittling away at long poles as if he were sharpening huge pencils, to make them pointed for spiking hay. The scene was bathed in cool sunshine. I looked toward the Big Scheidegg pass in the distance, which would lead me to the town of Grindelwald. Above the pass towered the sharp point of the highest Wetterhorn peak, cutting into a sky of feathery clouds.

The Wetterhorn was aloof, serene, regal; its Rosenlaui glacier resembled a giant fan sitting on the side of an enormous, gouged-out crater. The glacier, struck by the sun's rays, glittered; tracks of avalanches, the dark "folds" of the fan, contrasted with the whiteness of the ice. I abandoned myself to the view and to the crisp air, trying to assimilate the sight of this magic mountain. The Wetterhorn, as it generously gave its beauty to all mankind, seemed a fitting background for the Goldern school.

"The Wetterhorn," wrote Leslie Stephen, "is one of the most impressive summits in the Alps. It is . . . a long

and nearly horizontal knife-edge, which as seen from either end, has of course the appearance of a sharp-pointed cone." Stephen, a president of the British Alpine Club, climbed the summit and graphically described the experience:

"It is when balanced upon this ridge—sitting astride of the knife-edge on which one can hardly stand without giddiness—that one fully appreciates an Alpine precipice. . . . Behind you, the snow-slope sinks with perilous steepness towards the wilderness of glacier and rock through which the ascent has lain. But in front, the ice sinks with even greater steepness for a few feet or yards. Then it curves over and disappears, and the next thing that the eye catches is the meadow-land of Grindelwald, some 9,000 feet below. . . . The awful gulf which intervened between me and the green meadows struck the imagination by its invisibility. It was like the view which may be seen from the ridge of a cathedral-roof, where the eaves have for their immediate background the pavement of the streets below; only this cathedral was 9,000 feet high. Now, anyone standing at the foot of the Wetterhorn may admire their stupendous massiveness and steepness; but to feel their influence enter in the very marrow of one's bones, it is necessary to stand at the summit, and to fancy the one little slide down the short ice-slope, to be followed apparently by a bound into clear air and a fall down to the houses, from heights where the eagle never ventures to soar. . . . You are in a region over which eternal silence is brooding. Not a sound ever comes there, except the occasional fall of a splintered fragment of rock, or a layer of snow; no stream is heard trickling, and the sounds of animal life are left thousands of feet below. . . . The enormous tract of country over which your view extends—most of it dim and almost dissolved into air by distance—intensifies the strange influence of the silence. You feel the force of the line from Wordsworth—

The sleep that is among the lonely hills.

None of the travellers whom you can see crawling at your feet have the least conception of what is meant by the silent solitudes of the High Alps."

I turned to the peasant: "You are fortunate indeed to live here in sight of that fine mountain all year."

"Yes, yes," he said, carving away without looking up. "Nice mountain."

From Reuti I clambered down the mountainside through the meadows for two hours until I reached the Meiringen highway in the valley. From it a road branches toward Rosenlaui and the Big Scheidegg—one of the routes taken by the early pioneers to ascend the Wetterhorn. I had no ambition to climb that rugged peak; my plan was to take the Rosenlaui-Scheidegg road the next morning to look back from the Scheidegg pass toward Reuti, to look up to the Wetterhorn, and to look ahead to Grindelwald.

I had a fancier breakfast at the Hirschen Inn in Meiringen than a true *Wanderbursche* would have been able to afford, then followed up the road toward the Big Scheidegg pass, which separates the Meiringen and Grindelwald valleys. The tall trees stood on both sides of the winding road, a radiant day was unmistakably ahead, no deadlines, no pressures, nothing between me and the North Pole! For several precious hours I wandered in this world of my choosing, at my own pace, true to myself. "To journey on foot," says Rousseau in his *Confessions*, "in fine weather and in fine country, and to have something pleasant to look forward to at my goal, that is of all ways of life the one that suits me best."

I reached Rosenlaui and spent the night in a hostel only a few steps from the entrance to the Rosenlaui glacier gorge, a deep, narrow, churning gully, filled with melt water from the Rosenlaui glacier of the Wetterhorn. "Rosenlaui" seemed a strange word until I discovered that the *u* in -laui is a variant of *w*, and that *lauine*, occasionally found in older books, is merely an alternate form of *lawine*, avalanche. "Rosen," I doubt not, refers to the roseate glow of the glacier in the setting sun, the incomparable Alpine glow.

Farther along the trail toward Big Scheidegg I came upon Schwarzwaldalp, a meadowy plateau in awesome closeness to the "horns" of the Wetterhorn. As so many Alpine meadow plateaus, the Schwarzwaldalp, like the Seiser Alpe, seemed a self-contained world, although its tourist house there is supplied from Meiringen.

I stretched out in the grass, kept my eyes on the grotesque crags of the Wetterhorn; then continued leisurely until I reached the Big Scheidegg pass where the view changed with the suddenness of a movie cut: Ahead, and far down, was the Grindelwald valley; at about my altitude, extending northwest, was a lookout point called "First," connected by a chair lift with the town of Grindelwald; but as I looked back in the direction from which I had come . . .

There, in the distance, was the green shelf along which I had wandered only yesterday from the Brünig pass to Reuti. I could not see the chalet where the peasant had sharpened his mammoth pencils. I scanned the area where I knew it was, where I had looked toward Scheidegg (on which I now stood) at the base of the Wetterhorn. I narrowed my vision—there, somewhere, must be Reuti, and

somewhat to the side of it the École d'Humanité. I seemed to be tying the ends of a wreath now that I had completed my *wandern* around the Wetterhorn. The parts of the jigsaw puzzle fell into their slots. I was at home, here, where I had never been before.

A road sign told me it was an hour's walk back to Schwarzwaldalp, two hours to Rosenlaui, and four to Meiringen. It had been an easy stroll. I continued it for two hours in an almost straight line toward the First, my step sinking into the meadow and my eyes filled with the Wetterhorn, now presenting an angle different from that at Reuti. Yesterday it had glistened in the sun; today it threatened, glowering, in its jagged closeness, mysterious as Stonehenge.

When I reached the First I reached "progress" again; the summit terminus of the chair lift, the hotel, the white-uniformed waiters. On the viewing terrace, I ignored the hotel behind me and looked up into the face of the mighty, squatting temptress of Alpine rock-climbing aces, the Eiger.

Some mountains have extra willful individualities that impress themselves upon you. You see them only once and never forget them—just as some human faces impress their image into your consciousness. The Eiger was first ascended by an Englishman, Charles Barrington, in 1858. But its notorious north face resisted all attempts. This face is the highest cliff of the Alps, rising 5,400 feet straight from the Eiger meadows to the top—nearly twice the height of the 3,000-foot wall of El Capitan in California's Yosemite valley. Among the many tragic attempts to climb the north face of the Eiger—the Ogre—perhaps the most notorious was that by a team of two Austrians and two Germans in July, 1936. They managed to climb half way up the face the first day. Then one fell—the rope held but strangled him; a second fell and hurtled to his doom, pulling the third against a carabiner, where he froze to death. The fourth hung helplessly on his rope as rescuers came close enough to talk to him and to learn from him what had happened to the others; but the weather was merciless, and did not allow the rescuers to reach him, although they were only a single rope length below. The next morning, Toni Kurz too, was dead.

Two years later, in July, 1938, another team of two Austrians and two Germans succeeded. The climbs triggered a raging controversy over the merits of such suicidal enterprises that depend as much on weather, on luck, and on iron hardware as on iron will.

From the First I rode the chair lift down to Grindelwald. There, as in many Alpine resorts, I felt uncomfortably out of place. In Grindelwald, the Eiger north wall, which I had watched from the First, again stared directly in my face from one of the parking lots. There, telescopes were installed for the guests to watch the climbers. The fantastic railroad to the Jungfraujoch tunnels directly through the Eiger wall—the climbers scale past a window cut into it from which passengers can look outside. I wandered down the road past the last streetlight. It was now utterly dark. The outlines of the mountains vanished into blackness, and there was nothing between me and the stars. They dotted the sky in vast clusters—except for a single star. Not until morning did I discover that this lone star was the electric light from the Eiger tunnel.

The other triangulation points of my Oberland *wandern* —Schilthorn, Schynige Platte, and Lake Oeschinen— seem "archetypal" to me for the moods of man when he contemplates mountains: awe, the feeling of expanse, and the elementary mood of joy of life. These moods stem from views enjoyed by the wanderer at the end of a trail or cableway—not necessarily the highest vantage point in the area. A mood of this kind is different from that of a mountain climber who reaches the summit—the mood of the absolute, which had held me so intensely at the Zuckerhütl.

This classification is, of course, my own view of views. Once I asked a man just returned from the Alps how he liked them. "Well," he said, "there was just one damn beautiful view after another."

I reached the Schilthorn from Stechelberg, a township at the tip of one prong of a Y-shaped road system that begins at Interlaken. (At the tip of the other prong is Grindelwald.) I arrived at the 9,000-foot Schilthorn outlook on a day of exquisite sunshine. The view from the narrow platform made me choke up as the snowy white mantles of Eiger, Jungfrau, and Breithorn spread out in their brilliance. The world seemed an enormous house of worship, and I was not the first wanderer who had felt this. Near where I stood a plaque read: "Mighty and full of wonder are your works, O Lord." A Swiss flag fluttered in a lively breeze, hailing the beautiful world.

Suddenly fog wiped out the entire half-circle of the white mountain rampart before me, as if to remind me I should be grateful that I had the chance to see it. Nothing tantalizes the mountaineer more than to have worked his way to a fine view only to find it withheld by willful clouds. Sometimes the clouds reveal a fragment here and there, a glimpse of a celebrated skyline; at other times they do not oblige at all.

The fog, after its brief game, lifted from the Schilthorn, and the sharp relief stood out again in the sky.

The view from the Schynige Platte (6,450 feet), near Grindelwald, sparked a different mood. The cogwheel train from the Wilderswil station had first exposed views deep down into the valleys below, with their meadowlands and forests. Then, after a turn, the bridal white covering of the Jungfrau suddenly appeared—a virgin indeed, even though I could clearly see the railroad summit station Jungfraujoch. The Schynige Platte, unlike the narrow Schilthorn platform, is a broad plateau. From it the expanding view of Jungfrau, Breithorn, and a corner of Blümlisalp unfolded as I walked along. Seemingly within arm's length, these mountains glistened, pristine as if they had just been created. If I had been a spectator at the Schilthorn, here I was part of the scene, as the mountains clustered like friends. No religious tablet here—instead, a gaggle of singing schoolchildren.

Then on to Oeschinen Lake, which is on a high plateau reached from Kander valley. I let a chair lift take me from the valley to the plateau, and from there it was only a 20-minute stroll to the opaque, emerald lake. It is surrounded by a series of peaks, whose names end in -horn: Oeschinenhorn, Fründenhorn, Doldenhorn. All are dominated by the pointed Blümlisalphorn (12,044 feet), which I had already glimpsed from Schynige Platte. The friendly plateau with its lovely lake, trees, flowers, and wreath of mountains, seemed created as a playground for man, calling him to enjoy, enjoy, enjoy. I had a bursting awareness of being alive to experience this moment. Cattle grazed in the meadow, a small brook flowed to the lake. I walked to a "Sennhütte" for a delicious tumbler of cold milk.

Jean Jacques Rousseau's *Reveries of a Solitary Wanderer*, describes some lovely country scene by a Swiss lake as thrilling "for those solitary contemplatives who love to intoxicate themselves at leisure with the charms of nature, and to meditate in a silence disturbed by no sound except the cry of the eagles, the occasional twittering of birds, and the rolling down of torrents which fall from the mountain." Is Jean Jacques too sentimental for the jet age? For me he was good enough as I wandered along the trails of Switzerland. In the search for "happiness" and "peace of mind" his spirit lives in at least some wanderers in Europe, much as Thoreau's spirit lives among those in America to whom land is more than real estate.

"I was allowed to pass only two months [in that area]," Rousseau continues, "but I could have passed two years, two centuries, and the whole of eternity . . . I count these two months as the happiest time of my life."

Interlude

TO THESE DO WE BELONG

GASTON REBUFFAT

One of the greatest of mountaineers—"I know of no one more at home with the heights than Gaston," Wilfred Noyce writes in his preface to Mont Blanc to Mount Everest *(translated by Geoffrey Sutton, and drawn upon below)—is also the author of some of the most enjoyable books on mountaineering. It is a pleasure to know the ice and rock, the starlight and storm, and the warmth his prose and spirit bring down from his high world to ours.*

D.R.B.

That evening, when the sun dipped behind the earth, I experienced a deep feeling of serenity in the presence of so many natural things: the wood fire, the valley which drew us on, the magnetic mountains, the air of peace and silence, the living sky. I was happy to be there; and, thinking of my boyhood, of my very first excursion in the mountains, so like the one we were making now, I said to myself again: "It's just like the first time."

. . .

We had been lads of about fifteen. Our journey, which started in our native Provence, was to lead us to the foot of Mont Blanc. The sight of the Giant of the Alps! We had dreamt of it for years.

One morning we left the sea and set out for the heights. We rose with the sun, walked, stopped to look around, then set off again. Little by little we became bound in friendship with nature. The colours changed: we had not known that so many existed. Each day we discovered higher mountains, and so it was to continue to the end of our journey. We crossed tempting side-tracks, but we had set our course like sailors; it was towards Mont Blanc that we were headed, and at the thought of it our hearts beat faster. . . .

Every evening our happiness was the greater for feeling ourselves closer to our goal. The pilgrim who toils towards Mecca is happier than the shopkeeper of the Holy City.

Each of us had gathered some wood along the way, and for an evening our fire would illumine a hillock, a valley or a mountain corrie. With night, the high summits of the Oisans, then of Maurienne and Vanoise, seemed to draw closer, and one thought: "When I'm a bit bigger . . ." All was silence, yet one divined a mysterious life in the air and on the earth: the life of nature. Then came the cold; a light breeze tinted the embers; everything withdrew into itself and slept.

At last one day the narrow valley suddenly fanned out. The dream cherished for so many fervent evenings crystallized and took shape: there stood Mont Blanc, ideally beautiful.

. . .

Zugspitz platt toward Hochwarner and Karwendel chain

Watching waves break on a different shore, the poet Robinson Jeffers said: "It is only a little planet/But how beautiful it is."

Mont Blanc, France

Above all, mountains are silhouettes. They are cut out against the sky by the scissors of wind, frost and the centuries. This is how they first attract us.

Each has a time when it is particularly beautiful. This is never at noon, because at that hour all relief is flattened out by the light; rather it is at dawn or twilight, when the sunlight comes upon them or departs. What wide geniality is theirs in the morning when the sun's rays caress their ridges! How they soar towards the sky! And how abandoned, almost, they appear in the evening when the flaming sun falls behind the western ridges, as if the sky could support it no longer! . . .

Peaks are not only good to look at: they have a life of their own. Crowned with legends, they have names and stories that rouse echoes in our hearts and our imaginations. That is why these needles of rock, these eternal snows, so seemingly sterile, indifferent and useless, have called men to them, men who have tamed them though giving all, even their lives, to the deed.

As youths we needed a revelation; and on the mountains, fighting against the snow, the storm and the cold, face to face with silence, we seemed to be reborn.

. . .

Grossglockner toward Grossvenediger

The sun still rises in the east, and for nearly two centuries now mountaineers have been setting out to meet him each summer's day, after consulting the stars and the cold. The wind of good omen is still the North wind, and the climber still dreams whole winters through of some particular ascent.

Saussure, Whymper, Mummery, Cassin, major expeditions, or beginners going up the Petits Charmoz, Mont Blanc, Matterhorn, Grépon, Grandes Jorasses, McKinley, Alpamayo, Ruwenzori, Himalaya or little pinnacle of Provence—men in mountain parks created for their happiness. . . .

"Where there's a will there's a way" was as much the rule for de Saussure sweating under his perruque as for Mummery conquering the Grépon, as much for Comici caparisoned with pitons and étriers in the north face of the Cima Grande di Lavaredo as for Hillary and Tenzing scaling the roof of the world, all of them only stopping, like Regnard on his journey through Lapland, "where the earth went no further." . . .

Grey limestone or ruddy granite, ice of the gully or the serac, blown snow or snowy cornice, smell of rock, scent of flowers, delicate saxifrage or sub-Himalayan forest, starlight or storms, sun-scorched terrace, unreal frontiers, friendship between two being for better or for worse—to these do we belong.

Brenva glacier toward Mont Blanc, Italy

9. End of the Trail

I NEVER FORGOT my wish as an eighteen-year-old to see the Matterhorn, when I had been hitchhiking in its direction and wound up in the Dolomites instead. On my return trip, a generation later, I saw it; and on the same trip, Mont Blanc, highest summit of the Alps.

On that trip I again started from the eastern woodlands, then followed the Alps westward through Austria, and across the sweeping Arlberg pass to Zürich and Lucerne. Like sentinels the mountains looked down as I crossed the Four-Canton Lake to Flüelen; they closed in on the cogwheel train to Göschenen; and they opened up in a wide view from the top of Furka pass. Farther along the road I stopped near the Belvedere Hotel, at 7,600 feet, built on a crag directly alongside the incredibly bright blue Rhone Glacier where you can see the melted ice trickling down into the valley to become the Rhone River.

I arrived in Zermatt, the Matterhorn town, at midnight and went directly to a hotel without seeing The Mountain. Zermatt offers a peculiar mixture of fashionable tourist resort with palatial hotels and the original unsophisticated mountain village with ramshackle barns on the main street, from which the goats are driven to pasture (through the center of town) every morning.

I was aroused by their bells the morning after my arrival and went to the balcony to see what the jingling was all about. As I looked out I stared the Matterhorn directly in the face. I hadn't been thinking of it just at that moment, and the surprise was overwhelming. There is no mountain on earth like the Matterhorn. Its celebrated pyramid towered over the town and its picture-book church steeple. The white edges of the snow-covered mountain were set off sharply against the deep blue sky. I could understand instantly the sphinx-like fascination that peak had for the early mountaineers.

A cogwheel railway, built in 1898, the highest in Europe (10,200 feet), took me up to the Gornergrat with a panoramic view of the Matterhorn and its surrounding giants. There are people who see the Mona Lisa, listen to Bach, look at the Winged Victory and still feel no more than respect. When I think of the Gornergrat I find it hard to imagine that anybody, young or old, man or woman, American or Chinese, would not be stirred. Surely there cannot be many sights in the world to match it. I had felt this way when I first came upon the Grand Canyon; and I suppose one feels like this when first seeing the Himalayas from the south.

Nowhere have I felt my inadequacy of expression more than when I tried to make notes in my diary at the Gornergrat to describe what I saw; all adjectives seemed worn in the face of this, the finest mountain view I had ever seen—unsurpassed, I am sure, in the Alps, in Europe, and, probably, on the earth. I decided not to write anything and not to take pictures; I did not want to freeze my memory. I felt like the famous Swiss artist, Ferdinand Hodler, who would not paint the Matterhorn—it was too mighty, too awesome a subject to capture with a brush.

I confess I felt less frustrated when, later, I came across a well-accepted guidebook to Switzerland and discovered that its author, Eugene Fodor, also gave up when he came to talk about the Gornergrat, which "has inspired so many grandiloquent descriptions that it suffices to say here that it is indeed breathtaking to gaze over the shimmering surface of its glaciers."

I shall, then, merely sketch the physical setting of the Gornergrat: You stand on top of a high mountain on a platform that affords an unobstructed view all around. You are surrounded by a wreath of more than twenty "Viertausender." Every one of them has, like a symbol of its majesty, an ermine train, a glacier that flows down in a powerful yet graceful sweep. Many of the glaciers come together at the base of two or three of these mountains, forming medial moraines between them. The mountains carry names glittering in the history of mountaineering. Assembled here in a ring around you are Monte Rosa, the highest of all, 15,217 feet, half Swiss and half Italian; the mighty Lyskamm, 14,889 feet, the regal Breithorn, 13,685 feet, and many more. The Matterhorn, 14,782 feet, is not the highest, but it is by all odds the most arresting, and the *primus inter pares* in this illustrious company. It presents to the eye a main pyramid on which a small second pyramid, with a slightly tilted peak, seems superimposed; and it is this little extra twist that seemed to me the most telling characteristic of this peak.

As I hiked down during the afternoon, not taking the cogwheel train on the way back to Zermatt, the Matterhorn variously seemed to me like a sphinx, or like a rearing giant seal balancing an invisible ball on its nose, or like a watchdog. The last impression was especially strong, for the mountain seems to watch you all along the way as you descend; it peeks over the tops of the trees as you enter a forest, and it peers between the clouds when evening overtakes you. Sometimes the watchdog will growl when the storm blows the snow away from its nose in long horizontal streaks. Writers contemplating that heroic tilt have seen in it a sword blade pointing to the sky, a rearing horse, a tower in ruin, an obelisk, a torso, the Leviathan of Mountains, the Achilles of·the Alps . . . all fitting descriptions. John Ruskin called it the most noble reef in Europe.

It was late when I got back to Zermatt. I had seen the Matterhorn—thirty-eight years after I had been diverted to the Dolomites, and exactly one hundred years after it had first been scaled. The classic ascent of the Matterhorn in 1865 by the Englishmen Edward Whymper, the Rev. Charles Hudson, Douglas Hadow, and Lord Francis Douglas, two Swiss guides—Peter Taugwalder and son— and the French guide, Michel Croz, was such an event in the history of the Alps (and of mountaineering in general) that its centennial was observed as the "Year of the Alps."

In the evening, I looked out from my hotel window at it sitting there under the stars. I could well understand how Whymper felt—an artist who sketched the great Alpine peaks for a London publisher—when he wrote in his classic *Scrambles Amongst the Alps:* "Men who ordinarily spoke or wrote like rational beings, when they came under the Matterhorn's power seemed to quit their senses, and ranted, and rhapsodied, losing for a time all common forms of speech." Of the party of seven that reached the summit of the Matterhorn, four lost their lives. Only Whymper and the Taugwalders survived when Hadow slipped, on the way back, and the rope broke, in the most notorious tragedy of all mountaineering; the four fell to their deaths, 4,000 feet down the north wall. The ascent of the Matterhorn marked the end of the "golden age" of mountaineering—it could also be called the British age, because so many major peaks had first been scaled by British climbers and their Swiss guides. I had a sense of history as well as wonder as I gazed at the tilted summit for a long time during that starry night.

Some say that Austria has the loveliest part of the Alps, and Switzerland the most dramatic; France has the highest. It is only a short ride from Zermatt to Chamonix. And what the Gornergrat is to Zermatt, Le Brévent is to Chamonix. A daring two-section cableway lifts you from the town to the stark heights of a mountainous viewing platform. The first section goes up from Chamonix along the side of the mountain to one of its peaks. From there, the second section leads to a neighboring peak, Le Brévent, from which you get a magnificent view of Mont Blanc. In this peak-to-peak affair the cables are suspended in the air, like tightropes, and you sail along 300 feet above the treetops beneath.

This, then, was Mont Blanc, Zeus of the Alps, 15,782 feet high—4,810 meters—more than a thousand feet higher than Mount Whitney in the United States.

Like the Matterhorn, Mont Blanc has a rich history. I reflected on it as I faced the mountain. What jubilation there must have been on that memorable day, August 8, 1786, when the village doctor of Chamonix, Michel-Gabriel Paccard and his porter, the guide Jacques Balmat, stood at that mightiest dome of the Alps, the first men to do so. Horace Bénédict de Saussure, a Geneva professor of philosophy (which was then understood to include the natural sciences) had offered a prize for the discovery of a suitable route to the top. He wanted to explore Mont Blanc scientifically, and especially geologically. Mont Blanc, like the Matterhorn, had been shrouded in mystery —the mystery of all high peaks, held sacred by some of those who love the mountains most. "The tops of mountains are among the unfinished parts of the globe," said Henry Thoreau, "whither it is a slight insult to the gods to climb and pry into their secrets, and try their effect on our humanity. Only daring and insolent men, perchance, go there. Simple races, as savages, do not climb mountains —their tops are sacred and mysterious tracts never visited by them."

Paccard and Balmat found the route to Mont Blanc sought by the Swiss scientist. Dr. Paccard's achievement was ignored, and Balmat alone received credit, in part because Marc-Théodore Bourrit of Geneva, "the historian of the Alps," for personal reasons omitted Paccard's part in his account of the ascent. Later, Alexandre Dumas, who interviewed Balmat in 1832, perpetuated Bourrit's version. It was not until recently that Professor Graham Brown and Sir Gavin de Beer set the record straight in *The First Ascent of Mont Blanc*, a book chosen by the (British) Alpine Club to commemorate the centennial of the Alps in 1965. As a historic event, the reaching of the highest summit of the Alps by Paccard and Balmat is reminiscent of the conquest of Everest by Edmund Hillary and Bhotia Tenzing in 1953. Today, of course, ascending Mont Blanc in good weather is no problem for a reasonably well-trained tourist. It takes about six hours from the Aiguille du Goûter hut (12,467 feet) to the summit; and about eight hours from the summit down to Chamonix.

When I raised my eyes from Le Brévent to Mont Blanc I tried to picture the ecstasy experienced by Paccard and Balmat when they were standing on that white brow. I focused my gaze on the highest point and visualized them up there throwing their arms to the sky. Balmat later eloquently described his feelings: "I had reached the end of my journey. I had come to a place where no one—where not the eagle or the chamois—had ever been before." And in a final apotheosis: "Everything that surrounded me seemed to be my property. I was the King of Mont Blanc—the statue of this tremendous pedestal."

As I watched the now gentle-enough-looking pure white dome I realized why it was called the White Mountain. Unlike the Matterhorn, Mont Blanc does not stand by itself. "The tremendous pedestal" is part of a massif that it dominates—if the Matterhorn is a king among princes, Mont Blanc is a chairman in a directors' meeting. Grotesque, needlelike crags form the neighboring spires—L'Aiguille du Midi, L'Aiguille du Plan, L'Aiguille Verte. Angry banners of fog and clouds whipped the tops. Like a huge, white, gnarled index finger squeezed into a narrow vertical furrow between dark green forests, the Mont Blanc glacier probed deep into the valley where were clearly seen the tiny dots of Chamonix houses.

With my eyes I followed the glacier back up again from where it came, to the top of Mont Blanc.

In a sense, and at least for this most recent of my many return trips, this visit to the highest point of the Alps was "the end of my journey" too. It had started in the Vienna Woods with Schubert, and now it ended with Beethoven.

It became chilly and I slipped into my warm jacket as the wind began to blow. My eyes continued to rest on these beautiful mountains. This was the grand finale, and it filled every fiber of my consciousness. To be here was "right." This was what I wanted of life. I remembered a line by Ruskin: "The only days I can look back on as rightly and wisely spent, have been in sight of Mont Blanc, Monte Rosa, or the Jungfrau."

Those who have seen these mountains know what he is saying. I knew what he was saying. I adapted it for myself: "The only days I can look back to as rightly and wisely spent, have been in sight of the Alps."

The Last Islands

ARE THERE STILL wilderness islands in the Alps? The answer is yes if we accept the European meaning of the term: areas unspoiled by man, even though shelters (club huts) have been built and all peaks have been scaled. In the strict sense, as the term is used for sparsely inhabited parts of Asia, Africa, and the Americas, wilderness may be said to have ended when man discovered the beauty of the Alps. We have almost an "official" date for this discovery: the year 1729 when the Bernese surgeon-lawyer-botanist Albrecht von Haller published his book-length poem *Die Alpen*, glorifying the Alps. To be sure, he was not the first man to find the mountains attractive—Francis of Assisi in the thirteenth century, Petrarch in the fourteenth, and medieval German poets and writers all had praised the beauty of the Alps; and in the visual arts, Alpine motifs had appeared at the time of Albrecht Dürer. But in general man's attitude toward the Alps was still largely that of the Romans who had spoken of the *foeditas Alpium*, the abomination of the Alps. Since Roman times the mountains were feared and hated. Hunters, miners, worshippers (of the gods presumed to reside in their peaks), clerics, soldiers, and tradesmen who traveled through them did so because they had to. Only occasionally was a voice heard in the wilderness that sounded a friendly note. One such exception was Benedikt Marti, a professor in Berne, who wrote in 1557: "Who would not admire, love, and willingly visit the Alps? I should assuredly call those who are not attracted by them dolts, stupid dull fishes, and slow tortoises. I am never happier than on mountain crests, and there are no wanderings dearer to me than those in the mountains." He was a lone wolf. And it was not so much esthetic obtuseness that prevented his contemporaries from appreciating the beautiful heights and behaving like stupid dull fishes, but their fear of monsters. In 1723, Johann Jacob Scheuchzer, an honest-to-goodness natural-science professor in Zürich, wrote a "scientific" treatise about the dragons in the Alps—describing them, classifying them, and illustrating them. And why not? Had not reliable witnesses seen them? Did not the Lucerne museum show an authentic dragon stone, cut from a dragon's head? Weren't enough caves in the mountains, obviously the abodes of the dragons? As a youngster I walked many times past the huge "Lindwurm"—the famous dragon fountain at the market in Klagenfurt—never *quite* free of a shudder at the thought that such a monster might one day . . . when I was alone in the mountains . . . well, not really, but why was that fountain there and why all this talk?

Edward Whymper, as late as 1871, wrote in his *Scrambles Amongst the Alps* about the superstitious natives in the valleys around the Matterhorn: "gins and efreets were supposed to exist" at the Matterhorn, and "the wandering Jew and the spirit of the damned"; the natives spoke of "a ruined city on the summit wherein the spirits dwelt."

Although these fears persisted even up to Whymper's time, the fundamental and lasting change of attitude had come with Haller.

[continued on page 120

Interlude

THE WORLD WITHIN MYSELF

Interrelated selections by JAMES T. LESTER

The principals in the dialogue that follows, although somewhat apart in fields and quite apart in nationality, were almost contemporaries and not at odds at all in what they say here from their different vantage points.

José Ortega y Gasset was born in Madrid in 1883, studied at several leading German universities, and returned to Madrid in 1910 to become a professor of metaphysics. He is unique among contemporary philosophers in combining a remarkable lucidity of style, an enormous range of interest and knowledge, and a never-ceasing originality of thought. These data are from the publisher's material accompanying The Dehumanization of Art, *upon which Dr. Lester has drawn, a stimulating book indeed.*

*Geoffrey Winthrop Young, born in 1876, was one of the world's great mountaineers, was severely wounded in World War I but continued to climb and to prove, in the words of Sir Arnold Lunn, that "in the country of the mind, the one-legged man is king." * Mountain Craft *may be the book for which Young will be known best, but* On High Hills, *searched out here by Dr. Lester, "recreates scene, adventure, and emotional response in their original intensity and should communicate even to the inexperienced an understanding of the passion which makes men climb"—this the appraisal of anthologist W. R. Irwin in* Challenge.

James T. Lester was the psychologist with the American Mount Everest Expedition and a most capable photographer as well, as can be seen in Everest: The West Ridge (*Sierra Club, 1965*).   D.R.B.

I wish to go to latitudes where my life must become quite different to make existence possible, where understanding necessitates a radical renewal of one's means of comprehension, latitudes where I will be forced to forget that which up to now I knew and was as much as possible. . . .

I have never faced such overwhelming substance. . . .

One thing is certain: if the realm of the gods lies anywhere at all, it lies here. . . .

It seems to me that here no overwhelming imagination is required in order to invent overwhelming pictures. Formed by exaggeration, it forces others to exaggerate.

Here the greatest imaginations appear too small. . . .

It seems to me as though a thousand spirits were at hand, glistening like the eternal snows in the morning light, laughing gaily like lately waked children, confidential as if they had always known me, to strip my soul of all prejudices. Now they call me: Come! And they are running ahead of me into infinite space. . . .

There are still times in which I would like to be great in the earthly sense. But here, in the midst of this grandiose nature, no pettiness can abide. While I am looking out upon the snow-covered peaks . . . a nameless longing burns within me to get altogether beyond the limits of personal existence.

COUNT HERMAN KEYSERLING
(*writing of the Himalaya*)
The Travel Diary of a Philospher

At the Sella Pass, Dolomites

YOUNG:

Beside the lane up which we used to pass every day as children stood a school, with a belfry. The belfry was glazed with small panes of amethyst-coloured glass. Into and out of this floating sky-palace the folk of Fairyland flitted and sang. It was the playground for all the realities of a child's dream world. When I walk under it now, I see a vane and a box of pink glass, with some darker ruby panes, ill-matched but not unpleasing; they seem to blush for their past frailty, for the brittle charms that tempted and fell before the mischievous gravel from the boys' yard. The fairies, with the lights just catching the underside of their wings as they hovered across the pink sills, are all gone. But I can never pass the belfry without a catch of the breath, an involuntary hushing of the step.

. . .

Something has all but happened, or is all but going to happen when I have passed.
The fairies are waiting, only anxious to be again discovered; it is I who have moved off a little,
and can no longer quite see them. . . .

Mountains may have something of the same message, even for our later life. At night,
they seem to be waiting breathlessly, full of a rushing silence of unseen presences and of a
wondering curiosity as to whether we shall hear or see 'this time.' At moments when we are alone
or when we have in imagination 'put out a little from the land,' we can almost *feel* their
secret. But with the effort to shape it into words its meaning escapes us.

. . .

Snow crystals in Alpine meadow

Aggenstein near Pfronten in the Allgäu (German-Austrian border)

YOUNG:

The imagination of childhood does not analyze; it absorbs impressions in their entirety; and so, they last. Our maturer thought can accept no later inspiration without the microscope and the dissecting knife; and the poor thing, dried, classified, and planted out in some neat plot of memory, recovers no vigorous life, and soon fades. . . .

ERIC HELLER:

For the modern mind . . . has yielded to the inferior magic of facts, numbers, statistics, and to that sort of empiricism which, in its passion for concreteness, paradoxically reduces experience to a purely abstract notion of measurable data, having cast aside the 'immeasurable wealth' of authentic experiences of the spirit and imagination.

. . .

If I had not carried, through anticipation, the world within myself, I would have remained blind with my eyes wide open, and all search and experience would have been nothing but a dead and vain effort. (Truth is) a revelation emerging at the point where the inner world of man meets external reality. . . . It is a synthesis of the world and mind, yielding the happiest assurance of the eternal harmony of existence. . . .
There resides, in the objective world, an unknown law
which corresponds to the unknown law within subjective experience.

GOETHE (*quoted by Heller*)

ORTEGA:

The demagogues . . . who have already caused the death of several civilizations, harass men so that they will not reflect; manage to keep them herded together in crowds so that they cannot reconstruct their individuality in the one place where it can be reconstructed, which is in solitude.

La Meije from Col du Lautaret, France

YOUNG:

But through all these first active approaches to climbing, my inner feeling for mountains stayed a romance apart, unsocialized. I might often in a day visit the mountain realm in reading or in mind; but it was each time a deliberate withdrawal out of the daily round into a solitude. In thought, as in action, when it came, I could only find the full mountain delight under the 'blessing of the separate.'

. . .

Weathered tree, Hoher Göll, near Berchtesgaden

Mountains are a good adventure. They change little enough, in their attributes or in their charm, for us to consider them permanent. To their changelessness they owe the power of 'renewing our youth' whenever we are again among them. The same appearance, the same atmosphere, reproduce always the same feeling in us. We return at each sight of them to the self which first saw them, regardless of any change in ourselves. To this, too, they owe their comfortableness, their power, when we are among them, of making us see all other events of life in their right proportion. . . . It is upon their changelessness that we rely to give us back ourselves. That which is unalterable in them answers to that which remains unaltered in us, and restores it to its importance for us.

. . .

For me, too, our own hills, within the measure of my walking, are as lovely and as full of surprise as they ever were. Sometimes I even have the impression, when I see their lines in a new profile or combination, that they are now borrowing from the unattainable much of the enchantment which belonged to the unknown and the unattained, in the days of the last century when we first set out to explore among them, to discover new cliffs, to learn a new art of climbing, and—an inseparable part of the fascination of mountaineering— to find out something more about ourselves.

. . .

Romance, adventure, and the like, they are hackneyed terms, and we can all smile at them. But the spirit they describe is also laughably persistent among us; and when we are talking of mountains, and not of politics or ethics, we need not, happily, be continually rebottling the old wine of unrest in the terms of each new generation. It is, after all, a venerable spirit of adventure which drives us out to find, as we may, the discipline which alone can make a useful— or what once was called a manly—business of our short life. Progress, in the sense of change for the better, depends upon the survival among us of this unrestful spirit, and upon each individual finding for it a disciplined way of service.

. . .

The spirit of man, the product at once of his disciplined strength and of his disciplined thought, must prevail, and at all times, in the man, so that it may continue to prevail in the race of men; even although this may mean for the individual life the shortening by a few years of its single effort and example.

. . .

I began to recognize that, just as in mind I had always been alone with my mountains, so again now if ever I did walk or climb among them alone our intimacy took on a deeper meaning. It was no longer the admiring, half-jealous passion to possess, which had thrown a restless glamour over my school reading of alpine adventure. It had become a current of thoroughly masculine sympathy between us, forcible, intermittent, and provokingly attractive.

If any part of my attention were occupied with a human companion, with the consideration of an enjoyment other than my own, these mountains, I found, could assume an agreeable company expression, and were content to parade their heartiest conventions of formal charm and manner. If I approached them alone, although their complete intimacy continued tantalizingly to elude me, yet it was in a very different fashion. They were compelled to give ground, to yield up something of their confidences, now here, now there, a golden apple of mystery. . . . At moments it seemed certain that I should have captured their whole confidence round that cliff or over that summit, had not some distraction of steep rocks or some temptation of a new skyline been flung across my pursuit as an interruption to energy and purpose.

. . .

When we begin to notice how shy Nature is of company we are beginning to know a little about the natural world to which we belong. In any world which belongs to civilized humanity, in a crowd of town or school, Nature is moody if present at all, and she can behave as outrageously as Caliban.

. . .

In the open air, if mortals seek her with their human cross-purposes still uppermost in mind, if they 'hunt her in couples,' she will appear to envelop them with superficial sympathy, but elude them all the while with the secret misleading of a Puck. Only to those who walk alone by wood or sea or hill does she appear as Ariel, a sprite and fitful still, but a sprite in their occasional service; ready even at times to act as an interpreter of her own enchantments if the service they ask for is to be shown, behind the magic of form and colour, something of the principles of order and slower change that govern natural existences not made in man's image.

. . .

In these places, at these times, if we are alone, we may become aware of personalities in landscape and sound and motion as vivacious as our own but not humanly definable, and of new qualities of emotion manifested in them which burst through the poor wrappings of names which we give to them, anger or heartbreak or laughter, as through tatters of wet tissue-paper.

. . .

We do not feel proud enough of being alive. Things are so arranged as to convince us, during too much of our time, of their pettiness and of our own meanness. Our moral fibre suffers by our compulsory humility. As a tonic I know of nothing equal to a wide view from an unaccommodating ledge half way up a great mountain. It is more than a tonic, it is a vital elixir to discover how far the sense of our personal insignificance can be reconciled with a royal pride in the dignity of earth and in the successful imposition of our own will upon it.

Eastward the . . . downs rose, ridge behind ridge into the morning, and vanished out of eyesight into a guess; it was no more than a guess of blue and a remote white glimmer blending with the hem of the sky, but it spoke to them, out of memory and old tales, of the high and distant mountains.

J. R. R. TOLKIEN
Lord of the Rings

Waterfall near Hintertux, Austria

Tre Cime di Lavaredo, Dolomites, Italy

ORTEGA:

It is evident that man's destiny is not primarily contemplative; hence the best condition for contemplation cannot be to make it a directly intended, primary act. Only when it is confined to a secondary part, while the soul is moved by the dynamism of an interest, does our perceiving and absorbing power reach a maximum.

YOUNG:

Once the energy of the limbs, and of the restless mind, have found a common expression in that rhythm of great mountaineering, no lesser or separate outlet will content them. Let but our instinct and our physical experience alike tell us that the purpose to which our movement of self-realization is directed is a high and a healthful one, and all the poetry, all the reasoning, all the imagination of which we are capable, will fall ungrudgingly into step with our active pursuit, content with such share as may be theirs in the nearer pleasure, and in the remoter success, and unresentful of the discipline by the way.

ORTEGA:

Each one of us is always in peril of not being the unique and untransferable *self* which he is. The majority of men perpetually betray this *self* which is waiting to be; and to tell the whole truth our personal individuality is a personage which is never completely realized, a stimulating Utopia, a secret legend, which each of us guards in the bottom of his heart.

YOUNG:

There are many ways of climbing; and almost anything that is not naturally flat or artificially smooth can be climbed. Who shall say upon what character of surface, inclined at what angle, and continued to what height, any human climber will find his ideal? For each of us there is some appropriate kind of elevation, diverging at some suitable angle from the commonplace level, whereon we may be sure of coming face to face with the realization of our best selves as we struggle upward; and where we may note, if we have insight, how little or how great a distance still separates that fulfilled realization of ourselves from the spiritual heights which imagination can detect beyond.

ORTEGA:

This thing we call "civilization"—all these physical and moral comforts, all these conveniences, all these shelters, all these virtues and disciplines which have become habit now, on which we count, and which in effect constitute a repertory or system of securities which man made for himself like a raft in the initial shipwreck which living always is—all these securities are insecure securities which in the twinkling of an eye, at the least carelessness, escape from man's hands and vanish like phantoms. . . . The fate of culture, the destiny of man, depends upon our maintaining that dramatic consciousness ever alive in our inmost being, and upon our feeling, like a murmuring counterpoint in our entrails, that we are only sure of insecurity.

Heron, Murnau bog, Bavaria

YOUNG:

But our vivid and day-long consciousness of the mountain, of each other, and of the drama which we and the mountain played out at length together, cannot be faithfully reproduced. It has even escaped all but our own general recollection. The mountaineer returns to his hills because he remembers always that he has forgotten so much.

The Last Islands

[continued

Rousseau, the father of the French Revolution, is also the father of the Alpine Revolution. "There is something magical and supernatural in hill landscape," he said about a walk through the Alps, "which entrances the mind and the senses; one forgets everything else."

It is a tragic paradox that the first step in appreciating nature is also the first step in spoiling it. Of course, the early pioneers in the Alps are not responsible for the technological "developers" that followed them in the twentieth century. During the hundred years after Haller and Rousseau, peak after peak in this untouched wilderness was ascended by men who loved the mountains. By the middle of the nineteenth century, the Swiss had scaled Titlis, Dent du Midi, Jungfrau, Finsteraarhorn, Tödi, Sustenhorn, Piz Bernina, and other peaks; the Austrians, Grossglockner, Ortler, and Dachstein; the French, Mont Blanc, the Zermatt Breithorn, Mont Pelvoux; the Italians, summits in the Monte Rosa group. The British, until then, could only claim the Stockhorn and one of the Wetterhorn peaks, but theirs was the era that followed. Britons, jointly or solely, ascended many of the most coveted prizes in the Alps: Eiger in 1858, Aletschhorn in 1859, Blümlisalphorn in 1860, Monte Viso, north end of Monte Rosa, Lyskamm, Grosses Schreckhorn in 1861, Aiguille d'Argentière in 1864, Tschingelhorn, Mösele, and Matterhorn in 1865—the year that may be said to mark the end of the classical period of British mountaineering. It was also the British who started, in 1863, the world's oldest still-published mountaineering periodical, *The Alpine Journal*.

If Haller made the first lasting "ideological" dent in the Alpine wilderness, the practical penetration, begun by the pioneer climbers, was consolidated by the establishment of various Alpine clubs. The British Alpine Club, founded in 1857, was the first; it was followed shortly by the Austrian Alpine Club in 1862, the Swiss Alpine Club in 1863, and, within the decade, by the German, Italian, and French clubs. Now equipment was systematically tested. It had included strange items before: ladders (for climbing and for bridging glacial crevasses), ice drills, pocket clinometers, hand crampons, umbrellas, pistols to ward off eagles, and eye glasses with exchangeable lenses in different colors to vary the enjoyment of the scenery. In 1780, Baltasar Hacquet, a French-born Austrian professor, wrote a book, *Catechism for Mountaineers*, which included instructions for what to do with one's wig, whose

tail had a way of interfering with rock-climbing. The formidable early tools were poorly suited to scratch the wilderness; it was the rope, ineptly used before, and the sophisticated, modern climbing hardware, that changed the picture.

One important difference between wilderness as understood in the United States and natural condition as understood in the Alps is the existence of the club huts, as has been mentioned. The Alpine hut system, maintained by the national Alpine clubs, extends even into the glacial areas and into the national parks. Just as the Sierra Club maintains a system of huts in the High Sierra, so the Alpine clubs offer simple—in American terms often primitive—shelter to mountain visitors. The Alpine climber, ordinarily, carries no sleeping bag and usually no more food than he needs for the day. The nights are spent in shelters run by caretakers and supplied by horses, donkeys, and occasionally helicopters unless they are connected with the valley by cableways. Practically all ascents of high peaks are begun from the huts; if the tour cannot be negotiated in one day, the first day of the ascent is used to reach the hut, the next day to reach the summit.

Conservation groups in the Alps consider these huts legitimate aids to wilderness enjoyment rather than defilements of nature. The huts are built in rustic, practical style, many equipped with old-fashioned wood stoves, rough-hewn tables, benches, and bedsteads, and with pitchers and basins instead of running water. They are not hotels, but shelters against the (sometimes deadly) weather, aptly called "rifugio" in Italian. It is in the warm atmosphere of the lone huts, often in the glow of a kerosene lamp after a long day's hike, that companionship blossoms among those who make the effort to seek the quiet of the mountains.

In the United States huts are sometimes regarded as threats to the wilderness. The average mountaineer in the mild-weather Sierra Nevada sleeps outdoors and either carries his camping equipment and sustenance for several days on his back or, more frequently, has them carried by pack animals. These animals themselves need supplies, which must be carried by additional animals; I remember my surprise when I joined a wilderness trip and noticed a horse carrying an anvil, in the event that any horse might lose a shoe during the trip.

In 1966, when I prepared my Sierra Club friends for their first expedition to the Alps, one of the group leaders, a California physician, chairman of outdoor activities and accustomed to Sierra Nevada outings, gave me a hard time when he insisted that he was going to bring his sleeping bag, that he would sleep outdoors (not in the huts), and use mule trains in the Alps. If mule trains were not customary there for hikers, why should Europeans not learn something from us? Surely mules *could* walk in those mountains, couldn't they? I granted the possibility—after all, Hannibal used elephants. But the doctor was eventually persuaded to change his mind. Once there, he enjoyed his light sleepingbagless pack, his clean bunk in the huts, and the absence of mulishness.

Although huts, cableways, and automobile roads exist in the Alps, not to speak of villages and towns, you still can find large, unspoiled regions. They begin where the cableways, roads, and villages end, and this means primarily three areas: the dead-end valleys, the protected regions, and the areas of glaciers and winter snow in high altitudes.

All major Alpine valleys have dead-end side valleys, many rising to high altitudes, past small settlements, to the last village high in the mountains. It is the starting point to unspoiled areas.

However, many "last" villages no longer are the last. Take Obergurgl, highest Austrian "Kirchdorf" (village with its own church) in the Oetz valley. This gem of Tirol is the gate to fifteen isolated glaciated peaks, and a ski paradise in winter. Years ago when I drove from the Inn valley into the Oetz valley, the last section of the road to Obergurgl was a narrow, winding dirt road, braved by few. Beyond Obergurgl you were on your own. From there, wilderness lovers could climb to the glaciers, cross the crest of the Alps, and descend into Italy on the south side—into the sunshine of the Adige valley and the vinyards of Merano.

When I revisited Obergurgl recently, a paved widened road led all the way to the village; and just before the village, which is now a resort, a road sign read: MERAN, 61 KILOMETER. The road no longer ends at Obergurgl; it continues over the crest, past the glaciers, and into Merano, 40 miles away. It is a beautiful road all right, but the wilderness is gone. Obergurgl is no longer the last village in a dead-end valley, but one of the many settlements you pass on the road from the Inn to the Adige. Over the Oetz, an untamed, glacier-fed, rocky brook, adorned by thousands of miniature waterfalls, an automobile bridge passes three miles below Obergurgl. From the bridge, looking south and up into the mountains, you have one of those stunning views of a snow-capped crest which in the Alps are so bountiful; looking north, you see a garbage dump with millions of broken bottles and plastic cans, and all that insensitive man spills into Alpine brooks.

Every time a connecting road is built, two wildernesses are sacrificed—one on each side of the pass. Man keeps on building those connecting roads, in addition to dams and cableways. Mighty power stations now squat in many formerly remote valleys, and cableways lead directly to many glaciers—in some instances attacking the mountain from opposite sides, such as the two systems of the Dachstein.

And yet . . .

The side valleys in the Alps are as numerous as the legs of a centipede. Many are still untouched, and the awareness of the population and the momentum of conservation efforts are slowly growing. Western Austria and southern Switzerland have many places relatively unspoiled by bulldozers. Nothing useful would be served by being too specific, but the general areas can be indicated. The Bregenzer Wald near Lake Constance and, to the south, the Ferwall chain are still widely ignored by necktie tourists. This is true in spite of the auto roads—the Alpenstrasse in the German Alps, which skirts the Bregenzer Wald to the north, and the Silvrettastrasse, which passes south of the Ferwalls. Also happily ignored is much of eastern Tirol, an island separated from the main part by the Italian section of Tirol. Here the dead-end valleys of Tauerntal, Virgental, and Defereggental lead into the ice world of the Grossvenediger, twin of the neighboring Grossglockner. The famous Grossglocknerstrasse passes only 25 miles from the Grossvenediger as the crow flies, but in these valleys the hiker is still king.

In southwestern Switzerland, in the Canton Vallais, many lateral valleys of Rhone tributaries lead to unspoiled areas despite the closeness of resorts that lie at the foot of the Alps between the Matterhorn and Mont Blanc. The wilderness lover who leaves the last villages in the Bagnes, d'Hérens, d'Anniviers, and even Matter valleys will discover a world where the mountain boot has not yet given way to the rubber tire. In fact, the Swiss, combining love of nature with business sense, have either banned automobile traffic from many resort areas or deliberately have failed to build roads to them. In addition to Zermatt, such famed spots as Mürren, Wengen, Kleine Scheidegg, and others are so far safe from gasoline fumes.

In Italy, close to the most glamorous resorts of the Dolomites between Cortina and Belluno, are untouched areas, where cableways and chair lifts do not reach. The lower and less glamorous area of Carnia, the upper basin of the Tagliamento River, has a thick mantle of greenery—meadows alternating with beech and spruce woods—rarely visited by outside mountaineers. The lateral valleys of the beautiful Dora Baltea valley (with Aosta at its center), as well as Val Cogne, Val Savaranche, and the other side valleys leading to the Gran Paradiso massif, are still outside the main tourist stream, although they have been made accessible (originally by means of hunting trails for King Victor Emmanuel).

In France, the three major areas of the Alps—Savoy, Dauphiné, and Provence—are laced with side valleys in the upper Isère, Drac, and Durance rivers and their tributaries, all of which eventually flow into the Rhone. Even near the places of tourist attraction, in the Vanoise around the Col d'Iseran (Europe's highest automobile road, at 9,085 feet), in the Mont Blanc area around the Aiguille du Midi (with the world's highest cableway, to 12,605 feet), or in the Dauphiné around the Barre des Ecrins, are unspoiled islands. This also is true of the Maritime Alps, cunningly placed between the glaciers of the mountains to the north and the palm trees of the Côte d'Azur to the south.

Yugoslavia's share of the Alps is largely ignored by international tourists; almost untrodden game preserves (chamois, mountain cock, black cock) may be found in the northwestern corner of the country. The international visitor is usually found in the area around Bled, but the (locally well-known) areas near Lake Bohinj, the Kranjska Gora, and the Vrsic pass that leads into the beautiful Trenta valley are largely blank spots on the map for outsiders.

Immediately south of the Austrian Wörther Lake, an area teeming with tourists, is the Thury forest, part of a large forest area that reaches into Yugoslavia; it is as close to wilderness as anything can be in the Alps—the last bears of the Alps are said to have been seen there in recent years. When I visited this area in the thirties I was amazed by its primitiveness and isolation, only a few walking hours from the Wörther Lake resorts.

A hundred years ago, Leslie Stephen discovered an interesting quality of tourists—mostly British at his time—that preserved (although they could hardly take credit for it) much of the Alps: the sheeplike habits of the tourists. "During the last twenty years," he said in 1871, "Zermatt has been the centre of attraction for thousands of tourists. And yet, so sheeplike are the habits of the ordinary traveller, that these remote fastnesses still retain much of their primitive seclusion. Evolina, Zinal, and the head of the Turtman Thal are visited only by a few enthusiasts. . . . The tourist stream flows in its old channels, and leaves on either side regions of enchanting beauty, but almost as little visited as the remote valleys of Norway."

And, swinging at British customers of Cook's at St. Moritz, he wrote: "It is gratifying that a spontaneous process of natural selection [has taken place]. Like flies to like; the cockney element accumulates like the precious metal in the lodes of rich mines, and some magnificent nuggets may be found in and about St. Moritz; but luckily at no great distance may be found regions bare of cockneys . . . regions where the 'Times' is never seen, where English is heard as rarely as Sanskrit, and where the native herdsman who offers milk to the weary traveller refuses to take coin in exchange for it." Visitors were so rare in those side valleys that he was even worried or wondering about the innkeepers in those parts: "It is a mystery how the spiders which live in certain retired and, as we would think, flyless corners of ancient libraries, preserve their existence; but it is still harder to discover how innkeepers in these rarely trodden valleys derive sufficient supplies from the mere waifs and strays that are thrown, as it were, from the main body of tourists." Stephen's spoiled islands actually are spoiled strips of land. "The gregarious instinct . . . of the common-place traveller . . . leads migratory herds to spoil and trample underfoot some of the loveliest of Alpine regions . . . it draws them altogether into a limited number of districts, and leaves vast regions untrodden and unspoilt on either side of the beaten tracks."

The second group of unspoiled regions are the protected wilderness areas. The Swiss National Park in the Canton of Grisons is an example; after you leave Zernez, you leave the industrial age behind. Similarly, the French National Park protects the Pelvoux massif in the region of Dauphiné—lone ice fields on the Meije, Barre des Ecrins, and Ailefroide peaks, and valleys with untouched flora and fauna. In Austria, efforts are being made to turn a part of the Tauern chain with the Grossglockner into a national park, near a smaller area, south of the town of Mittersill, already protected. In Italy, Stelvio is not only a pass reached by an automobile road, but also a protected area of primitive wildness. And the national park surrounding Gran Paradiso (with its imposing peak of 13,223 feet), in addition to being a wild island for man, is the last refuge in Europe of the ibex that once roamed the entire Alps. This animal, now protected, is a goat, not an antelope like the chamois, and carries an impressive pair of horns, up to three feet long, slightly arched and rib-ridged—quite different from the small hooked horns of the chamois.

Private European conservation organizations are hampered by lack of funds and by public apathy, which is only slowly yielding. Unable financially to buy threatened areas, they lease them—such as the bird sanctuary of Neusiedler Lake at the Hungarian border. Public conservation is hamstrung by bureaucracy and lack of coordination, conservation in many areas being the responsibility of smaller political units (provinces, länder) rather than the national governments. Although the burden on conservation organizations and bureaus is heavy, their responsibility, because of the specific nature of the Alps as "man's own mountains" is broader than in the United States. The scope of conservation policy in the Alpine countries includes, in addition to the preservation of wilderness and wildlife, also the protection of such man-made objects as an old mill, an ancient peasant farm, even whole historical sections in cities. The medieval core of Salzburg is protected *as a whole*, not merely as individual buildings. In Tirol, builders are required by law to observe the traditional chalet style in the countryside.

The magnificent glacier zone of the Alps might be called the third of the unspoiled regions. Although many glaciers can now be reached by cableway and chair lift, once you set your feet on an icefield you are on your own. With proper equipment, competent guides, and good weather you can find solitude and fascination in a world of crystal glory. Glaciers have attracted the curiosity of scientists from Leonardo da Vinci to the Swiss naturalists Horace de Saussure and Louis Agassiz, and the admiration of nature lovers since the eighteenth century. The full enjoyment of glaciers, however, was not possible until they could be traversed on skis. Before skiing, many ice and snow regions were unreachable islands in winter. Now competent skiers may enjoy the glacial slopes, while low-slope skiing tourists are swarming in the village resorts. Today skiing is "democratized" and mechanized. Almost six hundred ski lifts carry skiers to Alpine heights, and a whole new hotel industry has grown up to serve their needs. In many places, the winter solitude is gone. Nevertheless, the ski lifts have not yet wholly taken over the role of the ski climber's sealskins among the many summits of the Alps. Even popular ski resorts can be the starting points for snow trips undisturbed by cables and machines.

The British played a decisive role in opening the "winter phase" of the Alps, just as they had opened the "summer phase." They were not the first, of course, to discover that weight distributed on two flat pieces of wood enabled you to climb in the snow and rewarded you with the pleasure of descent. The Norwegians had preceded the British and had ascended the Jungfrau on skis in 1895. But the British actually pioneered and popularized skiing in the Alps.

The Ski Club of Great Britain was founded in 1908, and Sir Arnold Lunn, "the Columbus of skiing," had the idea of sticking poles in the snow and snaking downhill between them. In 1922, together with friends, he established slalom ski-racing in Mürren. (His advisors included Hannes Schneider, the ski master of St. Anton in Tirol, who revolutionized the Norwegian skiing technique by inventing the crouching Arlberg style—a new way of stopping and of descending slopes.) Lunn was aware that skiing allowed man to enjoy the wintry solitude not accessible before. In his *Explorations of the Alps* he wrote:

"The Alps [owing to skiing] have taken a new lease on life. In summer the huts are crowded, the fashionable peaks are festooned with parties of incompetent novices who are dragged and pushed upwards by their guides, but in winter the true mountain lover has the upper world to himself. . . . Those who worship the Alps in their loveliest and loneliest moods . . . will climb in the winter months, when to the joy of renewing old memories of the mountains in an unspoiled setting is added the rapture of the finest motion known to man."

Among my most cherished recollections are those of my early ski adventures as a student. They include nightly expeditions down a mountainside to visit a young lady who inconsiderately lived in a valley, while I had found temporary winter employment in a mountain inn. Sliding down silently through the crisp snow in the translucent air under the stars was an eerie experience. Part of the run led through dense forest, so thick that on starless nights the darkness was nearly absolute. Almost total darkness is rarely experienced in our city lives, and is also rare in nature, where at least the outlines of trees or mountains are usually recognizable. Not so in my private nightly missions. A flashlight tied to my chest guided me through a narrow lane in the forest before I arrived in the valley under a certain window, where circumstances required that I climb in after I had buried my skis in the snow. (These were the same skis, with bindings of heavy metal brackets at toe and heel, that I brought to California years later; lifting them, together with hundreds of modern pairs, mostly aluminum, onto a conveyance called Magic Carpet, which runs from the road to the skiing area at Sugar Bowl, the busy attendant stopped when he got to my pair and asked: "Jeez, who uses *these* bear traps?")

It was on a less personal skiing expedition that I observed an avalanche at close quarters, near the mountain inn where I was employed. I went on a skiing tour with about twenty persons. We left early in the morning in order to cross a slope known to be exposed to avalanches.

[123

We moved slowly and single file, at considerable distance from each other, holding on loosely to a red nylon cord that would have made discovery easier if an avalanche really came down on us. In the cold morning, and generally on a cold day, the semi-frozen snow was considered safe, but we took extra precautions. If the sun came out later in the day and made the snow soggy and heavy, the danger would be acute.

We enjoyed our skiing that day in a safe terrain past the avalanche slope and got ready for the afternoon return. It had not been warm, and so we carelessly thought we could dispense with the single-file procedure. When we reached the avalanche slope we skied half-way down to a twenty-foot-wide ledge that intersected it. There we momentarily rested, standing up, leaning on our poles. Somebody pointed out the shape of the upper slope over which we had just come, and we all looked up, our ski tips facing the mountain side.

At that moment we heard dull rumbling, and instantly the whole slope seemed to be cataclysmically moving toward us. As far as we could see, the entire snow crust had detached itself from the side of the mountain on which it had rested and was slipping downhill, grotesquely exposing dull-green matted grass of last summer's growth. The spectacle was terrifying and hypnotizing as we watched the enormous mass come down rapidly, about to bury us in seconds. There was a moment of paralysis, at last broken by panic when somebody shouted, "Run downhill!" But we faced in the wrong direction! In a flash we jumped around, trying to point our skis downhill—only to get desperately entangled with each other. We had been standing too close, and we all fell, a squirming ball of skis, poles, arms, and legs, completely helpless. And down came the avalanche!

We were saved by pure chance. The avalanche came to rest in the ledge, settling and spreading against the slope, coming part-way. But the ledge was wide enough to leave room for us, although we were spattered by snow.

My most cherished skiing experience, however, is a Christmas Eve spent high up in a wintry Alpine hut with three friends. A beautiful day of skiing in the sunshine was behind us, we were tired but not weary. Still wearing our knitted sweaters we had our dinner around a heavy table in a corner of the hut. With much effort, somebody had brought a cake in his rucksack to be used for this occasion—a rare treat in a mountain hut. He stuck a small single candle in the middle—and that was our Christmas.

We were alone, each with himself, in our thoughts, yet close. We walked to the door of the hut and stepped outside into the snow, although we had taken off our boots and wore slippers. The snow was dry and crisp and did not melt in the few moments our slippers depressed it. A full moon was bathing our site and the surrounding mountains, all in deep snow, in almost phosphorescent light, infinitely beautiful. The silence was so absolute that I thought I could hear with my inner ear that vibration, that sound beyond sound, which surely must have been what led the ancients to the wonderful belief in the "music of the spheres"—the sounds of the heavenly bodies as they revolve in the universe. If, inside the hut, we did not have the customary tree that the occasion called for and no more than that single lighted candle, out there were trees by the thousands and the dome above was lit up by millions of lights.

The mountains formed endless ghostly waves in this silence that seemed to be of another planet; the slopes around us, which would be the lovely pastures of the Alps in the spring, were now under heavy snow, dipped in the magical light of the moon. We were standing side by side looking in the same direction into the night.

It is said that deep, lifelong friendships are cemented in the trenches of warfare, in the baptism of fire. Perhaps there is also a baptism of shared experience in nature. The friends of that night, more than a generation ago, are still my closest friends.

Many holy nights have passed since then, but none was as silent and meaningful. It is no coincidence that that simple tune was born, a century ago, in the same mountains, in the same snow, and under the same stars that were around us then. In the years that followed, when the dreaded Christmas tensions and obligations and done-to-death carols alienated me from my neighbors, I had the memory refuge of that night with my friends in the mountains. Whether in the meadows of the summer or the snows of the winter, at least I know where the place is that makes me wish for "time to linger." For this I feel so much richer. For this, as long as I live, I will always return to the Alps.

Letter to a Father

*I hope that I shall nowhere be found to have said 'Do as we did,' or even
'Don't do as we did'; but, somewhere or everywhere, 'Go and do something.'*

GEOFFREY WINTHROP YOUNG

YOU ASKED ME to read what you have written and to tell you what I thought of it. You are a romantic and you love your mountains as your own father did, and I, as the Grandson of the Alps in the family, share your feelings. You loved, left, returned to find the love undiminished, and saw it enhanced when your family loved the Alps too. You recall the myriad details of the experience—the Alpenrosen, the brooks, the fresh air, the tanned faces, the views from valley, pass, and summit. All these I share, and your recollections nail them into place.

You are pleased to escape the tourist traps and regret the passing of wildness in some of the valleys you knew. I am with you when you hang your head at the sight of new automobile roads to remote places, your disgust over the garbage dump in the Oetz Valley, your doubts about the new cableways to summits that formerly were the precious prizes of only those who earned them by their labors.

But you took that cableway to the Dachstein, and then what did you do? You sat down, picked up a piece of ice, and then looked through it as if it were a crystal ball to tell the past—your glacier trips in the past twenty-five years since I was born. But during that same time, Dad, something else has happened. In your beloved Austria alone the number of cable cars and lifts exploded from forty-four in 1945 to two thousand in 1970! That means two thousand solitudes gone, and this frightens me and angers me. I want to save the next two thousand—if there are that many left. I want a crystal ball for the future, not the past, but as things are going, I don't really need it— I can guess. You are looking at the helicopter on the Dachstein glacier and it bothers you as an invasion of its privacy, but it doesn't bother you enough. You see it as a mosquito, I see it as a bird of prey. You see the valley-connecting Timmelsjoch Road, and you are quite right in saying, with dismay, that it took two wild valleys off the list, the Oetz and Passer valleys; but the same happened when the Silvretta Road removed the isolation of the Montafon and Paznau valleys, and the Kühtai Road that of the Sellrain and Ochsengarten valleys, and so down the line for the length of the Alps, and while it is saddening to you, it is maddening to me. Yes, I know the new roads are beautiful, but the quiet valleys were more beautiful; the roads have enormous commercial benefits, but they are temporary and for a limited number of people, and the damage done is forever and for all mankind. I know

that the opposite is being said—that conservationists want to preserve the mountains for the privileged few who can climb them, for the young and physically fit; but if the many ruin nature, not even the few will have anything to enjoy in the future.

If I had my way I would just shout that we have had enough cement and wires, and that we should STOP NOW—cut our losses and leave the rest alone. I know this is radical and I know that thoughtful people have offered compromise solutions, and I'll come to them in a moment. I am a member of the student generation that has discovered that unless we shout no one will listen. We have shouted against the American war in Asia, repression at home, irrelevant education programs, and racism, and now we shout against the spoliation of nature, both in our own backyards and in the world at large. The beautiful thing about it all is that we have allies, and that although the war against the spoilers has, of course, not been won, the battles have at least started, and we are giving the builders and developers and money-makers a run for their money.

While you have been reminiscing, battles have been waged by the smallest communities up to the largest international organizations in the Alps. The lovely, tiny, remote Gauer Valley, a branch of the Montafon Valley in Vorarlberg was threatened to be reamed out by automobile traffic; the local community of the closest town, Tschagguns, despite the possible commercial benefits that added tourist traffic might bring, decided in a council meeting to close the road to vehicles; they put up a sign: NO AUTO TRAFFIC. FINE 10,000 SCHILLINGS. That did it. The journals of the Alpine clubs are filled with similar examples. At the other end of the scale, the International Alpine Commission (CIPRA—Commission internationale pour la protection des régions alpines), composed of delegates and government observers of the six Alpine countries, was founded in 1953 to fight for conservation; a delegate of the UNESCO commission for nature conservation takes part in their annual meetings. The commission is concerned with air and water pollution, road and cableway construction, new buildings, the two oil pipe lines that cross the Alps, Alpine aviation, and plant and wildlife protection. I enjoyed your telling the story of my Fritzi, Dad, but I want to know whether my kids will ever be able to find any aesculaps left in the Vienna Woods or whether all reptiles will be driven out by auto-

From Bayrischzell toward Grossglockner and Grossvenediger

mobile fumes or DDT. The International Alpine Commission has taken special interest in eagles and bears; in the past 25 years the eagles of France have been reduced by 70 percent—only 25 breeding pairs are left; in Switzerland and Austria 40 pairs each, in Bavaria 5; they are protected only in Switzerland and Germany. Bears, in addition to those that are said to have been seen in recent years at the Yugoslav-Austrian border, live wild, in small numbers, in the Brenta mountains in Italy; the local government has accepted the obligation of reimbursing anybody for damage done by these animals, which proved to be a simple and effective way of conservation.

Some national governments are waking up to the fact that wildlife uses no passports to cross borders. If a national park is near a border and the animals cross over the line, they can be hunted. The French, Italian, and Swiss governments have made regional arrangements, joining protected areas across the borders: The French, in 1963, created their first national park, La Vanoise, in the department of Savoy, directly adjoining the Italian National Park of Gran Paradiso, with a common border of five miles. The Italians, on their part, declared the Cancano valley, adjoining the Swiss National Park in the lower Engadine, a protected area, thus joining the Swiss park directly to the Italian National Park of Stelvio; the Swiss park was established in 1914, the Italian park in 1935, but it has taken until now to close the gap between them to strangle poaching. The Germans and Austrians are negotiating for a regional national park, which would combine the already protected Königssee area in Bavaria with the adjoining area of the Steinernes Meer range in Salzburg.

The national governments have established natural areas at various levels of protection—some permitting exceptions that undermine or nullify the protection promised on paper. Three countries have national parks in the Alps: the Italians have Stelvio and Gran Paradiso; the Swiss, the National Park in the Engadine; the French, La Vanoise—they are considering two more parks in the Alps: in the Dauphiné and Mercantour districts, and a third in the Cévennes (west of the Rhone). The Austrians have ambitious plans: the creation of the Tauernpark, to include the Grossglockner with the Pasterze glacier, the Grossvenediger, and the Krimml Falls—an area of 520 square miles (compared with 350 square miles of Yellowstone). The opening was planned for the European Conservation Year in 1970; but bureaucratic red tape among the participating länder of Tirol, Salzburg, and Kärnten, and the federal government, delays the project. (The German government opened the first German national park in 1970, but not in the Alps. The 50-square-mile Bayerischer Wald National Park, hailed as a "German Serengeti," is situated north of the Danube, near the border of Czechoslovakia, and reaches medium heights, up to 4,200 feet.)

If I had my way, I would stop all technical progress toward debasement from now on, and make an international park of the whole Alps, where the ibex of the Gran Paradiso and the bear of the Brenta roam freely again. If this is an unrealistic fantasy, what do the realists propose? It can be said in one word: Zoning. The International Alpine Commission has expressed its belief in this solution in various ways, and a number of spokesmen for that solution have outlined it in detail. Among them, Dr. Jean Dorst, Professor at the National Museum of Natural History in Paris, and Dr. Erich Berger, Chairman of the Munich Section of the German Alpine Club, are typical. Writing in a recently published book, *Before Nature Dies*, Dorst proposes totally protected zones, industrialized zones, and intermediate zones in which "fauna and flora can live side by side with man." Berger, writing in the German Alpine Club journal, similarly proposes a division of the Alps into three zones: "quiet zones," which include also the protected areas and in which all "development" is banned; "neutral zones," in which cableways and the like are not excluded in principle but subject to special scrutiny before permission to build them is granted; and "development zones," in which such projects "sensibly planned and carried out" are tolerated. A "horizontal" division into two zones was proposed in 1967 by the International Alpine Commission, at their annual meeting in Garmisch-Partenkirchen, in an effort to protect wildlife: they thought that in the entire Alps, regardless of national borders, wildlife should be protected above a certain altitude, for example above timberline. (The Swiss members were lukewarm about the idea. "In the vastness of the United States or in the Scottish Highlands such extensive wilderness areas may be possible," wrote the reporter who covered the conference, "but in Switzerland we can only protect specific mountain massifs or summit areas, by prohibiting roads, cableways, and buildings of all kinds except club huts. Our laws already have restricted the mountain-railway craze ["Bergbahnen-Baufimmel"] and restricted the number of airfields in the mountains.")

What does it all add up to, Dad? The wise men of today are no wiser than Leslie Stephen whom you quoted as saying, a hundred years ago, that tourists are like flies who aggregate at the same piece of cheese and don't go elsewhere. So why not make the best of a bad deal, write off what is gone and fight for what's left? If the fight is successful perhaps we can even recover some of the lost territory, too. But let's take one bite at a time.

Clearly, this is what conservationists in the Alpine countries are doing. The battles are on, but the enemy is strong. Who is the enemy and who are the friends?

The lines are drawn in some ways similar to those in the United States. The friends are primarily the Alpine clubs, the foes the industrial and commercial interests, especially the tourist-catering commercial interests in countries whose economies depend heavily on tourism. The government departments in whose jurisdictions the various aspects of conservation fall are "neutral" but largely subject to the pressures of the better-financed and better-organized industrial-commercial complex; a friendly government bias comes from the so-called "Naturschutzbehörden," the offices of conservation usually attached to the provincial (cantonal, länder) administrations. On the local level, the town or village councils are quite unpredictable, and a "good" mayor can do a fine job for conservation if he can carry his council under the device "we can't let them ruin our valley," but a "bad" mayor can succumb under the device "we'll all be rich if this road (dam, plant, cableway) is built." In Pontresina, Switzerland, the local council was actually joined by the local tourist bureau (usually a body much inclined to technical "improvements") in their unanimous rejection of a plan to build a cableway up Piz Palü. "The high mountains must be saved from cableways now and in the future," the resolution said, "we must preserve their unique and beautiful features undiminished."

Two cableway battles, both fought in the same general area, are case histories, illustrating how the lines are drawn and what outcomes may be expected in future battles. The first is the fight over the plan to build a cableway to the Watzmann peak in Bavaria. A Watzmannbahn Company was founded in 1968; it included the Tourist Office of Berchtesgaden, the local councils of Berchtesgaden and Ramsau, and private interests. Supporters were also the mayor and the head of the "Kurdirektion" of Berchtesgaden. With an eye on the Olympic Games in 1976, these parties promoted the plan of conversion of the Watzmann into a skiing area, although the mountain is in the heart of the protected nature area of Königssee, created in 1921 and since 1959 explicitly shielded against "cableways of any kind." The latter provision was particularly necessary, because an "exception" from the general protection of 1921 was granted in 1952, when the Bavarian Ministry of Transportation permitted the construction of a cableway (Jennerbahn). At that time, however, the Ministry demanded and received, as a condition for its permission, a written pledge from the county, local council, and Tourist Office of Berchtesgaden not to request any further cableways or an extension of the Jenner cableway.

Nevertheless, these bodies tried again in 1968. They ran into furious opposition from the German Alpine Club, which mobilized its members and the press. The representatives of the club made it clear that they were not opposed "in principle" to all cableways; in fact, their spokesman asserted that "mechanical climbing aids" ("Aufstiegshilfen"), as the official jargon calls cableways and ski lifts, are "indispensable" for skiers. It is clear that the Alpine Club subscribes to the "zoning theory," as outlined among others by Drs. Dorst and Berger. The club is not opposed to all cableways but wants to put the brakes on new construction in specific instances. "To permit a cableway at the Watzmann," said one club representative, "would be an irreparable violation of a remaining piece of untouched nature, for which later generations would curse us; we have to think of the future." He quoted the Official Bavarian Travel Office's admission that it was increasingly receiving requests from prospective visitors for information on "cableway-free" areas in which to spend restful vacations; he said cableways inevitably result in increased bus and automobile traffic with all its attendant disturbances.

The opponents of the plan found favorable reception by the press. The *Bayerische Staatszeitung* had even earlier editorialized that Bavaria had now enough Alpine cableways, and that the governmental conservation authorities should protect the remaining unspoiled mountains. (The comment was particularly well supported; Germany's part of the Alps is the smallest, with only 1600 square miles, but it had 58 cableways at the time of the controversy, almost as many as Switzerland and Austria taken together in a comparable area—Switzerland 43, Austria 21.)

The club pressure on the Bavarian Ministry of the Interior (as the highest conservation authority), the Bavarian Ministry of Agriculture (responsible for the grounds on which the cableway would have to be constructed), the Bavarian Ministry for Trade (responsible for authorizing cableways), and the government of Upper Bavaria (responsible for granting exceptions to the ban on cableways), ultimately led to the defeat of the plan. The German Alpine Club's accomplishment in preventing the project for the time being was motivated by its feeling of "grave responsibility," as the club journal wrote, "not merely for the interests of some mountain climbers, but for the preservation of an irreplaceable treasure belonging to all mankind for all time to come." On the other hand . . .

In the same land of Bavaria another battle over a "mechanical climbing aid" was lost. For years a controversy raged in Garmisch-Partenkirchen about whether to extend the Kreuzeck cableway to the Alpspitze, to reach the coveted Osterfelder ski slopes. The German Alpine Club, aided by the tourist club "Naturfreunde," fought this plan, too. But this time the commercial interests were supported more strongly by the skiing enthusiasts than in Berchtesgaden. The construction has begun.

These examples show the division that rends the ranks of the mountain lovers themselves. The same Alpine Club member who as a climber loves the solitude of a peak in the summer may as a skier want the lift in the winter. The leadership of the Alpine clubs that rely on the zoning theory must weigh in each case whether to approve or oppose a new construction plan. Their (perhaps temporary) victory over the Watzmann plan may have been facilitated by the fact that the Watzmann is not an ideal ski mountain for family use, and could only be made into one by extensive cuts into the forest. The leadership, also, is sensitive to the charge of being, as a group, comparable to a "white-haired old man opposed to every mechanical device," as the club's spokesman said in the Watzmann controversy.

But what a club cannot do, in view of the ski and skilift enthusiasts in its own ranks, unencumbered conservationists can do freely. If the uncommitted *Bayerische Staatszeitung* could say, unequivocally, as far back as October 29, 1965, "we've enough cableways," conservationists at large could at least try for the whole pie, while supporting, in the meantime, the preservation efforts of the zoning theorists. Although the examples were drawn from the Bavarian Alps, the problem, with the booming ski population, is of course Alps-wide. The most recent example, at the time of writing, is an effort by "developers" in the French Alps to build high-rise ski resorts in the Thorens valley near Mont Blanc. They are planning a resort to accommodate 40,000 visitors, making it one of the biggest in the world; the number of skiing Frenchmen has soared to an estimated two million from only 400,000 a decade ago—every one of them a potential spender in a hotel or user of a ski lift; hence French conservationists are not optimistic about their chances of thwarting this effort. They are particularly dismayed about the developers' intention of including in their schemes 6,000 acres of the adjoining national park of the Vanoise, 5 percent of the park's total area—a glacier that would allow summer skiing, and whose annexation, they claim, is vital to the venture.

The French Alpine Club is appalled. "What are we

headed for?" asks one of its spokesmen, "Pizza parlors on the top of Mont Blanc?" The park is a wildlife sanctuary, say conservationists, that doesn't even allow motorized vehicles. Building ski lifts and inviting thousands of skiers could be disastrous.

Here, as in the Watzmann case, public opinion is aroused, the press is sympathetic to the foes of the developers, and the conservation organizations are moving. The French federation of conservation societies, augmented by a number of other organizations, in a conference held in the Museum of Natural History in Paris, violently denounced the plan in a press conference that attracted national attention. They specifically called for an investigation of the motives of the developers.

A battle of a different kind, this time in Italy, has been raging over the plan to build a part of the Autostrada Alemagna, the freeway between Munich and Venice, through the lovely Valle di Sesto (Sextental), near the celebrated Tre Cime (Drei Zinnen) turrets, one of the finest spots in the Dolomites. The first stage of the battle was won when a press campaign cut loose against the originally contemplated route from the Piave valley via Cortina d'Ampezzo northward. Cortina won, the freeway plan was changed—but conservationists fell from the frying pan into the fire: now a viaduct, supported by 180-foot cement posts, is to span the Sexten valley and mar the view of the Sexten mountains. Spearheaded by World War I ski hero Luis Trenker, the local council of Sexten, the Italian Alpine Club, the South Tirolean tourist federation, and other bodies are urging the public inside and outside Italy to flood the Italian authorities with protests and to urge them to reroute the freeway from Auronzo to Misurina, San Candido, Dobbiaco, which would be more expensive but less ruinous to the Alpine scene.

In Austria, the Alpine club journal *Bergsteiger* has been trying to awaken the public to the consequences of a projected electric power plant in the Nassfeld valley near Badgastein. This Bockhartseewerk would dry out the entire valley as far as Böckstein, including a fine local water fall. It's an uphill fight, because the very government office supposed to protect nature, the Salzburg provincial government (as conservation authority), has declared its sympathy for the plan.

An example of a battle of yet a different type could be cited from Switzerland. There conservationists, primarily from Swiss Alpine Club circles, are turning against the ever-growing noise produced by mountain aviation, largely helicopters used by "parlor mountaineers" ("Salon-Bergsteiger") and skiers with fat pocket books. Switzerland has already 42 mountain landing strips. Conservationists have been protesting that in one respect planes are even worse than skilifts—their noise penetrates mercilessly even the most secluded valleys.

As I reflect on these examples culled randomly from recent newspapers and journals, on the battles about noise, power plants, automobile roads, high-rise buildings, cableways, and "development" of skiing areas, I can draw only one conclusion, Dad: If you want me, and those after me, to share in your idyllic Shangri-las and Christmas ski vacations as you described them, very unidyllic battles are inevitable. In these battles the national Alpine clubs are the conservationists' strongest and sincerest and most dedicated allies. Yet the appeal of conservationists must go to the public at large, if a full commitment to "so far and no farther" is what we want.

In 1970, The Council of Europe observed European Conservation Year and issued a sweeping Declaration of Conservation in Europe. The statement included among other provisions the principles of an ecologic point of view in harmony with economic and social advancement; and proposals of general political guidelines for regional and local conservation, for public enlightenment and education, and for all-European cooperation.

It is good to see that the Council stresses the vital tool the public must have for the defense of the remaining islands: the law. It is to buttress over-all national planning and international cooperation. The recommendations of the Council should do much to encourage a wider scope and more resolute enforcement of national laws. The Swiss have been leaders in conservation legislation. In 1962 they voted with an impressive majority for a constitutional provision that gave the cantons jurisdiction in conservation matters; charged the federal government with taking into consideration conservation when pursuing its tasks; and gave the federal government the authority to regulate plant and wildlife protection. In 1966 the law based on the constitutional provision passed; it spelled out the areas in which the federal government was to give special consideration to conservation when "pursuing its tasks." Those areas broadly included the planning and construction of federal railroads, national high-

ways, energy plants, and permission to clear forests. Of particular importance is the provision for a federal inventory of all objects to be preserved; these are placed under special protection by the federal government.

All Alpine countries have conservation laws, of course, but they have holes in scope and enforcement. Nevertheless, the Council of Europe has a solid basis on which to construct a larger, firmer, better-coordinated House of Conservation.

As I look ahead, I see battles still larger than those about railroads, cableways, and wildlife. Battles will also have to be fought against water and air pollution, traditional-design power plants, and, above all, about population control. I read in the newspapers that the bacteria count of the Alps-born Rhine is 10 per cubic centimeter at its source in Switzerland, and 1,500,000 when it enters Holland after flowing through the German industrial centers; last year chemicals poured into the Rhine killed forty million fish. The battle for waste- and sewage-processing plants will have to be fought on a wide front. The drying up of the Alpine streams and waterfalls by power plants may finally come to a halt through their replacement by atomic plants if we can solve the waste-disposal problem. And the beginning of the world-wide battle against overpopulation will need our tenacious support not only to save the Alps, but the planet.

Although these are literally battles of survival of the human race, they are desperately hard because they are directed not only against the greed of the few but also against the apathy of the many. Dr. Hans Palmstierna, a famous Swedish environmental expert, has said: "I am afraid, a real disaster may have to occur before people will realize the utter necessity of environmental control."

In conclusion let me, the "realist," tell you, the "idealist," of a dream: It is the dream of the Alps of the future, from the Mediterranean Sea to the Hungarian plains, as beautiful as you knew them in the past, shielded from further spoliation. It's a strange dream because it can come true only if we don't fall asleep. I, for one, promise I won't.

Berkeley, California   ANTHONY KNIGHT
July 20, 1970

If our adventure had been a good one, of the kind that lasts, and we have followed it undazzled by the sparks of our own achievement, we shall be more occupied with the thought of the persistence of the star than with regret at the surrender of our own torch. Not less than our pleasure in caring for something greatly, is our pleasure in knowing that others will continue to care for the same thing as greatly, and in the same way.   GEOFFREY WINTHROP YOUNG

Epilogue

PURE NOTE IN THE SILENCE

There I lay staring upward, while the stars wheeled over. . . . Faint to my ears came the gathered rumour of all lands: the springing and the dying, the song and the weeping, and the slow everlasting groan of overburdened stone.

J. R. R. TOLKIEN
Lord of the Rings

It was vast, Titanic, and such as man never inhabits. Some part of the beholder, even some vital part, seems to escape through the loose grating of his ribs as he ascends. He is more lone than you can imagine. There is less of substantial thought and fair understanding in him than in the plains where men inhabit. His reason is dispersed and shadowy, more thin and subtile, like the air. Vast, Titanic, inhuman Nature has got him at disadvantage, caught him alone, and pilfers him of some of his divine faculty. She does not smile on him as in the plains. She seems to say sternly, Why came ye here before your time. This ground is not prepared for you. Is it not enough that I smile in the valleys? I have never made this soil for thy feet, this air for thy breathing, these rocks for thy neighbors. I cannot pity nor fondle thee here, but forever relentlessly drive thee hence to where I *am* kind. Why seek me where I have not called thee, and then complain because you find me but a stepmother? Shouldst thou freeze or starve, or shudder thy life away, here is no shrine, nor alter, nor access to my ear.

HENRY DAVID THOREAU
The Maine Woods

In the wilderness life seems neither long nor short, and we take no more heed to save time or make haste than do the trees and stars. This is true freedom, a good practical sort of immortality.

JOHN MUIR

Weathered tree with Gehrenspitze, near Reutte, Tirol

That evening my mind went back to the brilliant patches of aspen which here and there, for no apparent reason, seemed to be successfully disputing the mountain slopes with the more prevalent evergreens, and I wondered why. Some people think it is better to leave such questions alone and to take the beauty of nature for granted. If sufficiently phlegmatic they may take the attitude of the legendary English visitor who refused to see anything wonderful about all the water which tumbles over Niagara, because, as he asked, "What's to prevent it?" Some of the more philosophically inclined may, like Wordsworth, object to what he called "peeping and botanizing." But there are others—and I am among them—who find themselves seeing it more vividly when nature is not merely a spectacle but a phenomenon interpretable in terms of the infinitely complex and subtle processes of which the spectacle is an outward and visible sign. And I have never found either the beauty or the wonder diminished.

J. W. KRUTCH
Grand Canyon Today and All Its Yesterdays

How glorious a greeting the sun gives the mountains! To behold this alone is worth the pains of any excursion a thousand times over. The highest peaks burned like islands in a sea of liquid shade. Then the lower peaks and spires caught the glow, and long lances of light, streaming through many a notch and pass, fell thick on the frozen meadows.

JOHN MUIR
The Mountains of California

Pelvoux massif with Pic Gardiner and Le Dome, France

Lake Kochel toward Herzogstand and Heimgarten massif, near Murnau

Through all this tangled skein of earthly life must run the golden thread of beauty. Beauty is everywhere; we need not go to the hills to find it. Peacefullness is everywhere, if we make it so; we need not go to the hills to seek it. Yet because we are human and endowed with physical qualities, and because we cannot divorce ourselves from these qualities we must utilize them as best we can and seek through them beauty that we may return refreshed in mind and spirit. So we go to seek beauty on a hill, the beauty of a larger freedom, the beauty that lifts us to a high window of our fleshy prison whence we may see a little farther over the dry dusty plain, to the blue ranges and eternal snows.

FRANK S. SMYTHE
Valley of Flowers

Virgen valley, East Tirol, looking toward Lasörling

Will civilization grind out of man all his ancient qualities, his fierce unreasoning passions, his hopes and fears, his love of nature and primitive things? Does peace and security spell effeminacy and deterioration of the virile qualities? What will we become when the need to struggle for our existence is banished from the perfect world promised us by philosphers, economists and pacifists? Perhaps in this a reason is to be found for all forms of physical adventure. The qualities that have given us domination over the beast, that demand safety not as a dead level of existence but in opposition to danger continue to find an outlet for their activity in sports labeled dangerous, useless, or unjustifiable. Peace between men is not incompatible with maintenance of physical virility when so many adventures are possible in the open air. Whether it be cricket or rugger field or the heights of the Himalayas there is enough to satisfy this adventurous spirit of ours without resort to the soul-deadening work of killing our fellow men. It remains to be seen how our inherited instincts are to be adapted to our need of peace and happiness, the two things men crave most. I am sure myself that they are to be found in the open air, and that the present movement in this direction, not only in Britain but in many other countries, is an unconscious revolt against the primeval desire to kill in order to maintain physical safety and virility and represents the growth of the human intelligence toward a new and happier conception of the universe and human relationships.

F. S. SMYTHE

The need is not really for more brains, the need is now for a gentler, a more tolerant people than those who won for us against the ice, the tiger, and the bear.
The hand that hefted the ax, out of some old blind allegiance to the past, fondles the machine gun as lovingly. It is a habit man will have to break to survive,
but the roots go very deep.

LOREN EISELEY

142]

Alpenrosen (Rhododendron hirsutum)

CONRAD GESNER,

PHYSICIAN, SENDS HEARTIEST GREETINGS
to the most distinguished doctor,
JACOB AVIENUS.

 I HAVE determined for the future, most learned Avienus, so long as the life divinely granted to me shall continue, each year to ascend a few mountains, or at least one, when the vegetation is flourishing, partly for the sake of becoming acquainted with the latter, partly for the sake of suitable bodily exercise and the delight of the spirit. For how great the pleasure, how great, think you, are the joys of the spirit, touched as is fit it should be, in wondering at the mighty mass of mountains while gazing upon their immensity and, as it were, in lifting one's head among the clouds. In some way or other the mind is overturned by their dizzying height and is caught up in contemplation of the Supreme Architect. Those, to be sure, whose spirits are sluggish wonder at nothing; they remain idly at home, do not enter the theatre of the universe, hide in a corner like dormice in the winter, do not consider that the human race has been established in the world in order that from its marvels it might infer a something greater, namely the Supreme Divine Will itself. With such sloth do they toil that like swine they are forever staring at the earth, never gazing with uplifted face at the heavens, never holding aloft their countenances to the stars. Let such, therefore, wallow in the mire, let them lie stupefied amid gains and sordid pursuits. The followers of

5

[A page from the Grabhorn Press book, on *The Admiration of Mountains*. The unfinished sentence ends positively: "The followers of wisdom will proceed to contemplate with the eyes of the body and the spirit the sights of this earthly paradise: among which are by no means of least account the steep and lofty slopes of mountains, their inaccessible precipices, the hugeness of their flanks stretching to heaven, their high crags, their dark forests."   D.R.B.]

In other years, these recurring visions of great peaks, cloud-girt in space, homelands for all the gods of our fancy, have never failed to kindle each of their own fresh wonder, their own renewed excitement: Olympus, a rolling tableland of snow drifting above a haze of lilac coast and sea; Mont Blanc from the Val Veni, a moonlit spire framed in a grey corona of glacier and traveling mist; Snowdon on an arctic evening, a white cone far out against the sea, with the red sword-rays of sunset about its summit. But that first sight, the hidden promise on the snows of Glaramara, joined hands across the amazement of the moment with the dreamland of the past. I was again a boy, possessed with the shapes of an imagined alpine world. Nor was that all the revelation which the mountains purposed for this moment. The road, unaccountably, became a lane, between towering hedges in place of the hills; and above, in mid-sky, the snows flamed suddenly into a cupola of pink glass, out of which something strange and friendly from fairyland was just going to appear, for me alone.

The wind from those snows of Glaramara, from the dream-heights of boyhood, from the fairy palaces of childhood, blew upon a tide of longing for greater glacial peaks which had been rising steadily and imperceptibly during all the years of unconscious preparation. At its breath the first wave—of full, conscious recognition, and of resolve— crested and broke. For over fifty uneasy, happy years the wind has blown challengingly, and the waves of response have crested and swept against it ceaselessly, to break upon this mountain range, now upon that; and although among the chances of life they have spent something of their force and frequency, time has brought no stilling of the desire, no hungering for calm.

GEOFFREY WINTHROP YOUNG

In his laborious efforts to attain mountain tops where the air is lighter and purer, the climber gains new strength of limb. In the endeavour to overcome obstacles of the way, the soul trains itself to conquer difficulties; and the Spectacle of the vast horizon, which from the highest crest offers itself on all sides to the eyes, raises his spirit to the Divine Author and Sovereign of Natures.

POPE PIUS XI

Space, and the twelve clean winds of heaven,
    And this sharp exultation, like a cry, after the slow six
    thousand steps of climbing!
This is Tai Shan, the beautiful, the most holy.

Below my feet the foot-hills nestle, brown with flecks of green;
    and lower down the flat brown plain, the floor of earth,
    stretches away to blue infinity.
Beside me in this airy space the temple roofs cut their slow
    curves against the sky,
And one black bird circles above the void.

Space, and the twelve clean winds are here;
And with them broods eternity—a swift, white peace, a presence
    manifest.
The rhythm ceases here. Time has no place. This the end
    that has no end.

Here when Confucius came, a half a thousand years before
    the Nazarene, he stepped with me, thus into timelessness.
The stone beside us waxes old, the carven stone that says:
    "On this spot once Confucius stood and felt the smallness of
    the world below."
The stone grows old:
Eternity is not for stones.
But I shall go down from this airy place, this swift white peace,
    this stinging exultation.

And time will close about me, and my soul stir to the rhythm
    of the daily round.
Yet, having known, life will not press me so close, and always I
    shall feel time ravel thin about me;
For once I stood
In the white windy presence of eternity.

                                        EUNICE TIETJENS

How many more generations will pass before it will have become nearly impossible to be alone even for an hour, to see anywhere nature as she is without man's improvements upon her? How long will it be before—what is perhaps worse yet—there is no quietness anywhere, no escape from the rumble and the crash, the clank and the screech which seem to be the inevitable accompaniment of technology? Whatever man does or produces, noise seems to be an unavoidable by-product. Perhaps he can, as he now tends to believe, do anything. But he cannot do it quietly.

. . .

Perhaps when the time comes that there is no more silence and no more aloneness, there will also be no longer anyone who wants to be alone. If man is the limitlessly conditionable creature so many believe him to be, then inevitably the desire for a thing must disappear when it has become no long attainable. Even now fewer and fewer are *aware* of any desire to escape from crowds, and most men and women who still make traditional excursions to beach or picnic grounds unpack their radios without delay and turn on a noise to which they do not listen. But it is not certain that this is not a morbid appetite rather than one which has become normal or that it, any more than any other morbid appetite, brings real satisfaction when it is gratified.

. . . Only after they began to be scarce, only after the natural rather than the man-made, and solitude rather than company had to be sought after, did the great empty spaces become attractive, or indeed, other than alarming. Man's place in nature was precarious long before the situation was reversed and it became nature rather than man whose survival seemed uncertain.

JOSEPH WOOD KRUTCH
Grand Canyon and All Its Yesterdays

Until one is committed there is hesitancy, the chance to draw back, always ineffectiveness. Concerning all acts of initiative (and creation), there is one elementary truth, the ignorance of which kills countless ideas and splendid plans: that the moment one definitely commits oneself, then Providence moves too. All sorts of things occur that would never otherwise have occurred. A whole stream of events issues from the decision, raising in one's favour all manner of unforseen incidents and meetings and material assistance, which no man could have dreamt would have come his way. I have learned a deep respect for one of Goethe's couplets:

Whatever you can do, or dream you can, begin it.
Boldness has genius, power, and magic in it.

. . .

On each day's march we were to find the day made memorable either by some little incident, almost always trivial, or by a sight so briefly seen that we could not have imagined that any indelible record would be left on the memory. But so it was. We moved daily through scenes of the most splendid beauty; daily, on every hand and wherever we might turn, there it was manifested, so that we became familiar with beauty and took its presence very much for granted, and ceased consciously to respond: until that daily, fleeting glimpse into the heart of beauty's very self came suddenly upon the inner eye—flashed upon the soul—and was gone. The duration of vision is of no consequence.

. . .

These were the magic days, each one yielding an especial enchantment. There was the morning when we turned out to find the world wrapped in the silvery-grey of cobwebs: all the fields, every bank and shrub, veiled by spiders' lacery, drenched with dew and shining in the low sun. There was the night on the hill-top at Barechina, when the full moon hung over the forest; and the evening at Didihat when we were granted our last sight of the snows. The clouds rose off the spires of the Panch Chuli, as always they used to do at the sunsettings when we watched from our tents by the glaciers. But now as never then we saw the slender summit leap like a flame from the Five Fires, lightening the darkness of the cloud pall. While there are men alive to read that sign in the skies, the mountain will draw their hearts . . . and the sacrifice will be offered, and will be accepted, and the expedition will set out.

W. H. MURRAY

I am being driven forward
Into an unknown land.
The pass grows steeper,
The air colder and sharper.
A wind from my unknown goal
Stirs the strings
Of expectation.

Still the question:
Shall I ever get there?
There where life resounds,
A clear pure note
In the silence.

DAG HAMMARSKJOLD
Markings

Natural park, Murnau bog toward Ester mountains

Mühlsturzhörner and Grundübelhörner near Berchtesgaden

We seek a renewed stirring of love for the earth;
we urge that what man is capable of doing to the earth
is not always what he ought to do;
and we plead that all people, here, now, determine that
a wide, spacious untrammeled freedom shall remain

. . .

Geiselstein, Ammei mountains, Germany

as living testimony that this generation, our own,
had love for the next.

D.R.B.

Remember thy creator in the days of thy youth.
Rise free from care before the dawn, and seek adventures.
Let the moon find thee by other lakes,
and the night find thee everywhere at home.
There are no larger fields than these,
no worthier games that may here be played.
Grow wild according to thy nature, like these
sedges and brakes, which will never become English hay.
Let the thunder rumble; what if it threaten ruin
to the farmer's crops? That is not its errand to thee.
Take shelter under the cloud, while they flee to carts and sheds.
Let not to get a living be thy trade, but thy sport.
Enjoy the land, but own it not. Through want of enterprize and faith
men are where they are, buying and selling,
and spending their lives like serfs.

HENRY DAVID THOREAU

Bog cotton, Bernina area, Switzerland

Friends of the Earth in the United States, and sister organizations of the same name in other countries, are working for the preservation, restoration, and more rational use of the earth. We urge people to make more intensive use of the branches of government that society has set up for itself. Within the limits of support given us, we try to represent the public's interest in the environment before administrative and legislative bodies and in court. We add to, and need, the diversity of the conservation front in its vital effort to build greater respect for the earth and its living resources, including man.

We lobby for this idea. We work closely with our sister organizations abroad, and with new and old conservation organizations here and abroad that have saved so much for all of us to work for.

We publish—books, like this, and in smaller format—because of our belief in the power of the book and also to help support ourselves. Our environmental newspaper is "Not Man Apart."

If the public press is the fourth estate, perhaps we are the fifth. We speak out for you; we invite your support.

Friends of the Earth Foundation, also in San Francisco, supports the work of Friends of the Earth and organizations like it with projects in litigation and in scientific research, literature, and education.

Publisher's Note: The book is set in Centaur and Arrighi by Mackenzie & Harris Inc., San Francisco. It was lithographed and bound by Arnoldo Mondadori Editore, Verona, on coated paper made by Cartiera Celdit and Bamberger Kaliko Fabrik. The design is by David Brower. The Layout is by Kenneth Brower.